Ex Libris

Shakespeare's Sonnets

and

A Lover's Complaint

The texts of the Arden Edition
edited and introduced by
Katherine Duncan-Jones

AS

Arden Shakespeare

1 3 5 7 9 10 8 6 4 2

This edition of *Shakespeare's Sonnets*
first published in 2010 by Methuen Drama

Arden Shakespeare is an imprint of Methuen Drama

Methuen Drama
A & C Black Publishers Limited
36 Soho Square
London WID 3QY

www.methuendrama.com
www.ardenshakespeare.com

A CIP catalogue record for this book is available
from the British Library

ISBN 978 1 408 12898 5

Designed and typeset by Country Setting, Kingsdown, Kent
Printed and bound in Great Britain by Clays Limited

❧ Contents ❧

❦ Preface ❦

In the Elizabethan period, substantial collections of sonnets –
'sonnet sequences' – normally concerned love. Most of them
offered ingenious variations on a single theme: a male speaker's
intense devotion to a beautiful, virtuous and unattainable
lady. The speaker's love is idealised and apparently free from
physical desire. Elizabethan sonnet sequences thus belong
broadly to the mediaeval tradition of 'courtly love'. This
tradition originated in feudal societies in Southern Europe, in
which, by praising the beauty and chastity of their lords' wives
in complex and ingenious verse, gifted courtiers indirectly
showed their loyalty to the lords themselves. Like many of
their Italian and French predecessors, Elizabethan English
sonneteers used fictitious names for their love-objects –
'Stella', 'Delia', 'Licia', 'Phillis', 'Idea'. Some also gave fic-
titious names to their male speakers, such as 'Astrophil' or
'Parthenophil'.

   Shakespeare's sonnet sequence is quite different. Although
most of these 154 sonnets can be broadly described as con-
cerning love, the great majority do not seem to be addressed to
a lady, but to a young man of high rank. He is quite often
called 'my love', as in Sonnets 40, 63, 66, 89 and 99. Once,

in the poem numbered 126 that closes the 'fair youth' group, he is addressed as 'my lovely Boy'. Only twenty-eight of Shakespeare's sonnets, those numbered 127 to 152, are clearly addressed to a woman or women. Sentimentalising Edwardian critics and biographers started a practice of referring to this woman as 'Shakespeare's Dark Lady', and the phrase has never quite gone away. However, she doesn't sound at all lady-like, despite a single sonnet (128) in which she plays on the virginals, a high-class keyboard instrument that was a forebear of the piano. She is not conventionally beautiful, nor is she chaste. In the celebrated Sonnet 130, beginning 'My mistress' eyes are nothing like the sun', the speaker boasts of being perfectly contented with a mistress who is neither beautiful, fragrant, nor graceful, unlike the ladies praised to skies by other poets. In subsequent sonnets in this segment, such as 134–8, it seems that she is not merely unfaithful to the speaker-lover, but exceptionally promiscuous. And rather than invent-ing pretty names either for the love-objects celebrated in his sonnet sequence or for himself, Shakespeare used both of his own real-life names, while leaving the objects of his or his speaker's love apparently nameless. The title of the sequ-ence as a whole, which there is every reason to suppose was both arranged by the poet and published by his wish, is *Shake-speare's Sonnets*, and in the 1609 edition the title is repeated at the top of every right-hand page.

For earliest readers, therefore, the book provided constant reminders that the sonnets printed below the title are

'*Shakespeare's*'. And in Sonnets 135 and 136 the speaker puns repeatedly on 'Will' (short for 'William'), and closes with the lines:

> Make but my name thy love, and love that still;
> And then thou lov'st me, for my name is Will.

It is hardly surprising that many critics and biographers have viewed the Sonnets as personal, even confessional, and that many have been deeply embarrassed by them, especially during periods when same-sex love has been viewed as abhorrent, even criminal. The more Shakespeare came to be elevated as England's 'National Poet', the more problematic it became that his Sonnets, apparently highly personal, were so deeply unconventional as love poems. Shakespeare's elevation was physically manifested in the elegant statue of him placed in Poets' Corner in Westminster Abbey in 1740, and it is telling that there was very little interest in the Sonnets in this period. One eighteenth-century editor, George Steevens, claimed that they could not and should not be published, while others, including Samuel Johnson, never mentioned them. Though William Wordsworth claimed, in old age, that 'with this key / Shakespeare unlocked his heart', the Sonnets were generally ignored, or mentioned only with embarrassment, during the nineteenth century. Sir Sidney Lee, one of the best Shakespeare scholars of the late nineteenth/early twentieth century, claimed that the sonnets had been published surreptitiously, without the poet's knowledge or permission. Other scholars suggested that they had been published by Shakespeare's enemies out of deliberate malice, so damaging were they to his personal reputation. We should remember that this was also the period during which Oscar Wilde both expressed open admiration for the Sonnets, and endured imprisonment and disgrace for his own homosexual relationships.

Only from the mid-twentieth century onwards have the Sonnets come into their own, being at last widely read and appreciated. However, a lively debate continues about whether they should be read as having things to tell us about Shakespeare's own emotional and personal life, or whether they should simply be analysed and appreciated as powerful and exciting poems.

Published in 1609, Shakespeare's major sonnet sequence appeared early in the reign of James I, a monarch whose delight in the company of handsome male courtiers was immediately noticed. By this date most of Shakespeare's plays had been written, apart from the so-called 'late romances'. But he probably composed sonnets throughout his life. He always used what is known as the 'English', or 'Shakespearian', form of the sonnet, made up of three four-line units with alternate lines rhyming, abab, cdcd, efef, followed by a concluding couplet, rhyming gg. At least eight sonnets in this form are incorporated into Shakespeare's plays. Most concern romantic love in the conventional, heterosexual, sense. One of the loveliest is spoken by Romeo and Juliet when they first meet at the Capulet ball, and culminates in their very first kiss. Some other sonnets in the plays are rather different, such as the Prologue to *Romeo and Juliet*, providing a concise plot summary in perfect sonnet form. In the late tragic-comedy *All's Well that Ends Well* the heroine, Helena, sends a letter to her mother-in-law written in sonnet form.

Turning to the sonnet sequence that you are about to read: a single one, numbered 145, seems to have been written very early. The words 'hate' and 'away' in line 13 can be read as a pun on Anne Hathaway's surname, sometimes pronounced 'Hattaway'; and the phrase that opens the closing line, 'And saved my life', can be read as 'Anne saved my life'. This is perhaps not one of Shakespeare's best sonnets. It is rather unusual both in being written in short lines, with four strong stresses rather than five, and in telling a little story. It may be the earliest piece of Shakespeare's verse that we have, being written in the summer of 1582, when, aged only eighteen, he was courting the slightly older Anne Hathaway, who was a few months pregnant by the time of their marriage in November. However, the story of the large collection eventually published in 1609 begins many years later.

In a survey of contemporary English writers published in 1598 a man called Francis Meres mentioned and praised, in addition to a dozen of Shakespeare's plays and the narrative poems *Venus and Adonis* (1593) and *Lucrece* (1594), 'his sugared sonnets among his private friends'. The word 'sugared' suggests that these were lyrical love poems, but the phrase 'among his private friends' may indicate that Meres himself hadn't been lucky enough to read these sonnets for himself. The first two sonnets to reach print, versions of those later published as 138 and 144, certainly concern love, but they are far from sweet, or 'sugared', in tone. They were included in a tiny collection of poems attributed to Shakespeare called *The Passionate Pilgrim* (1599). In the sonnet later numbered 138 the speaker explores a sexual relationship based on lies. The man pretends to believe that the woman is faithful to him, although he knows she is not, while the woman pretends to believe that her lover is young, even though 'she knows my days are past the best'. Sonnet 144 is even more unusual, and, for most readers, even more unpleasant. The male speaker is torn between 'Two loves', one 'a man right fair', the other, and 'worser', 'a woman coloured ill'. Things become even more complicated when the speaker suspects that his 'bad angel', the woman, has tempted his good one, and given the young man a sexually transmitted infection. We are a long way away here from the world of *Romeo and Juliet*, Shakespeare's most popular play until he wrote *Hamlet*.

In their later versions these two sonnets are placed within the so-called 'Dark Lady' segment of the sequence, 127–52. All of the 'Dark Lady' sonnets seem to have been written relatively early, perhaps in the early-mid 1590s – the same glorious period in which Shakespeare also wrote such plays as *Romeo and Juliet* and *A Midsummer Night's Dream*. It is rather shocking to reflect that at the time when he was writing so sympathetically about the pains of young love Shakespeare was also, in private moments, writing about the brutal force of male lust (see, especially, Sonnet 129) and female promiscuity. However, apart from the two sonnets which reached print in 1599, the rest seem to have been efficiently kept away from wider scrutiny until Shakespeare felt that the moment had come to go public. Because he divided his time between London and Stratford, and also sometimes went on tour with his acting company, Shakespeare was no doubt in the habit of keeping his valuables, including work in progress, securely locked up. An image of locking valuables away before making a journey occurs in the first line of Sonnet 148.

The main body of the Sonnets seems to have been written from the late 1590s to the early 1600s. This has been shown through detailed study of words, phrases and images that occur both in Sonnets 1–127 and in datable plays. But they are unlikely to have been written in the order in which they appear. They were composed at various times and in various places, being finally revised and arranged shortly before their publication in the summer of 1609. There was a good practical reason why Shakespeare decided to finalise and publish his sonnet sequence just then. Because of prolonged and severe outbreaks of plague in London the public theatres had been closed for more than a year. For Shakespeare, both a leading member of the King's Men acting company and a major shareholder in the Globe Theatre on the Bankside, this was an economic disaster. In this period authors of books received no royalties from sales. However, Shakespeare will have received substantial one-off payments both from Thomas Thorpe, the publisher of *Shakespeare's Sonnets*, and from the mysterious Master W.H., the man to whom the book was dedicated

The sonnets placed first, 1 to 17, form a coherent unit. In every one the speaker presents reasons why the person addressed – beautiful, young, talented and nobly-born – should marry and produce children. Sonnets 3, 13 and 16 indicate that this person is male, and imagery in other sonnets reinforces this. The preceding dedication of 'THESE. ENSUING. SONNETS.' to a 'Master W.H.' strongly hints that the patron might be the young nobleman in question. The likeliest real-life original is William Herbert, Third Earl of Pembroke (1580–1630). In his late teens and early twenties Herbert was notoriously reluctant to marry, rejecting several brides proposed by his family. He also got into trouble with the Queen for making Mary Fitton, one of her Maids of Honour, pregnant, and then refusing to marry her. His reluctance to marry, combined with his evidently vigorous sexual desire, suit the addressee of 1 to 17. Another piece of circumstantial evidence is the dedication of the 'First Folio' of Shakespeare's plays (1623) to William Herbert and his younger brother. Shakespeare's long-term colleagues Heminge and Condell report that the Herbert brothers had known Shakespeare, and had been generous patrons to him. However, we still lack decisive proof that William Herbert was indeed 'Master W.H.'. Like many issues arising from *Shakespeare's Sonnets* the identity of 'Master W.H.' will be the subject of debate for the foreseeable future.

The central body of the *Sonnets*, from 18 to 126, touch on many themes: love, friendship, beauty, transience, the human ageing process, betrayal and forgiveness, poetry itself. All seem to be addressed to, or else to concern, both 'love' as an emotion, and 'love' in the sense of a person loved. As in 1–17, when the sex of the person addressed is indicated, it is male. But in this great central sequence-within-a-sequence Shakespeare's imaginative and creative scope is wonderfully wide. Most readers will find poems here that they will want to read and re-read many times, whether reflections on Time, such as 18, 19, 60, 64, 65; on the ageing process, such as 19, 22, 63, 73; on betrayal and disappointment, such as 33, 34, 35, 57, 58 – or many other themes of timeless fascination.

Many Elizabethan sonnet sequences were rounded off with a poem of 'complaint', usually in the voice of a female speaker, in contrast to the male voice of the sonnets. Though Shakespeare's sonnets are unlike those of his contemporaries in many other ways, his sequence does resemble theirs in this respect. In 1609, *A Lover's Complaint* was introduced with its own title and attribution. It is 'BY / WILLIAM SHAKE-SPEARE'. Recent studies suggest that it was probably written fairly soon after *Hamlet* (1601/2). In it, a nameless maiden is seen weeping and throwing love-letters and jewels into a river. She tells her story – or delivers her 'complaint' – to a sympathetic old man. She has been seduced by an irresistibly charming young man of high rank, who has deserted her. Much though she longs to free herself from her obsession with him, she cannot. In its vivid evocation of landscape, clothes and objects, as well as of emotions, *A Lover's Complaint* is strikingly different from the sonnets which precede it. For readers in 1609, who could not see *Hamlet* performed because the theatres were closed, it provided a piquant reminder of that fascinating tragedy, and especially of the figure of Ophelia, cruelly cast off by Hamlet, and her watery end. For readers today, especially perhaps female readers, it provides a refreshing antidote to the 'maleness' of the *Sonnets*.

Katherine Duncan-Jones
Oxford

❧ Shakespeare's Sonnets ❧

TO.THE.ONLY.BEGETTER.OF.
THESE.ENSUING.SONNETS.
MR.W.H.ALL.HAPPINESS.
AND.THAT.ETERNITY.
PROMISED.
BY.
OUR.EVER⁄LIVING.POET.
WISHETH.
THE.WELL⁄WISHING.
ADVENTURER.IN.
SETTING.
FORTH

T.T.

❧ I ❧

FROM fairest creatures we desire increase,
  That thereby beauty's rose might never die,
But as the riper should by time decease
His tender heir might bear his memory:
But thou, contracted to thine own bright eyes,
Feed'st thy light's flame with self-substantial fuel,
Making a famine where abundance lies,
Thyself thy foe, to thy sweet self too cruel.
Thou that art now the world's fresh ornament,
And only herald to the gaudy spring,
Within thine own bud buriest thy content,
And, tender churl, mak'st waste in niggarding.
  Pity the world, or else this glutton be,
    To eat the world's due, by the grave and thee.

❧ 2 ❧

WHEN forty winters shall besiege thy brow,
  And dig deep trenches in thy beauty's field,
Thy youth's proud livery, so gazed on now,
Will be a tattered weed of small worth held:
Then being asked, where all thy beauty lies,
Where all the treasure of thy lusty days,
To say, within thine own deep-sunken eyes,
Were an all-eating shame and thriftless praise.
How much more praise deserved thy beauty's use
If thou couldst answer, 'This fair child of mine
Shall sum my count, and make my old excuse',
Proving his beauty by succession thine:
  This were to be new made when thou art old,
  And see thy blood warm when thou feel'st it cold.

❧ 3 ❧

Look in thy glass, and tell the face thou viewest
   Now is the time that face should form another,
Whose fresh repair if now thou not renewest
Thou dost beguile the world, unbless some mother.
For where is she so fair whose uneared womb
Disdains the tillage of thy husbandry?
Or who is he so fond will be the tomb
Of his self-love, to stop posterity?
Thou art thy mother's glass, and she in thee
Calls back the lovely April of her prime:
So thou through windows of thine age shalt see,
Despite of wrinkles, this thy golden time.
   But if thou live remembered not to be,
   Die single, and thine image dies with thee.

❧ 4 ❧

UNTHRIFTY loveliness, why dost thou spend
   Upon thyself thy beauty's legacy?
Nature's bequest gives nothing, but doth lend,
And being frank, she lends to those are free:
Then, beauteous niggard, why dost thou abuse
The bounteous largesse given thee to give?
Profitless usurer, why dost thou use
So great a sum of sums, yet canst not live?
For having traffic with thyself alone,
Thou of thyself thy sweet self dost deceive;
Then how, when nature calls thee to be gone,
What acceptable audit canst thou leave?
   Thy unused beauty must be tombed with thee,
   Which used, lives th'executor to be.

THOSE hours that with gentle work did frame
　　The lovely gaze where every eye doth dwell
Will play the tyrants to the very same,
And that unfair which fairly doth excel.
For never⁄resting time leads summer on
To hideous winter, and confounds him there,
Sap checked with frost and lusty leaves quite gone,
Beauty o'er⁄snowed and bareness everywhere;
Then were not summer's distillation left,
A liquid prisoner pent in walls of glass,
Beauty's effect with beauty were bereft,
Nor it, nor no remembrance what it was.
　　But flowers distilled, though they with winter meet,
　　Leese but their show; their substance still lives sweet.

❧ 6 ❧

THEN let not winter's ragged hand deface
  In thee thy summer, ere thou be distilled:
Make sweet some vial, treasure thou some place
With beauty's treasure, ere it be self-killed.
That use is not forbidden usury
Which happies those that pay the willing loan;
That's for thyself to breed another thee,
Or ten times happier, be it ten for one:
Ten times thyself were happier than thou art,
If ten of thine ten times refigured thee;
Then what could death do if thou shouldst depart,
Leaving thee living in posterity?
  Be not self-willed, for thou art much too fair
  To be death's conquest and make worms thine heir.

7

Lo, in the Orient when the gracious light
Lifts up his burning head, each under eye
Doth homage to his new appearing sight,
Serving with looks his sacred majesty;
And having climbed the steep-up heavenly hill,
Resembling strong youth in his middle age,
Yet mortal looks adore his beauty still,
Attending on his golden pilgrimage:
But when from high-most pitch with weary car
Like feeble age he reeleth from the day,
The eyes, fore-duteous, now converted are
From his low tract, and look another way:
So thou, thyself out-going in thy noon,
Unlooked on diest, unless thou get a son.

Music to hear, why hear'st thou music sadly?
  Sweets with sweets war not, joy delights in joy;
Why lov'st thou that which thou receiv'st not gladly,
Or else receiv'st with pleasure thine annoy?
If the true concord of well‑tuned sounds
By unions married, do offend thine ear,
They do but sweetly chide thee, who confounds
In singleness the parts that thou shouldst bear:
Mark how one string, sweet husband to another,
Strikes each in each by mutual ordering,
Resembling sire, and child, and happy mother,
Who all in one, one pleasing note do sing:
    Whose speechless song being many, seeming one,
    Sings this to thee: 'Thou single wilt prove none.'

❧ 9 ❧

Is it for fear to wet a widow's eye
   That thou consum'st thyself in single life?
Ah, if thou issueless shalt hap to die,
The world will wail thee like a makeless wife;
The world will be thy widow, and still weep
That thou no form of thee hast left behind,
When every private widow well may keep,
By children's eyes, her husband's shape in mind:
Look what an unthrift in the world doth spend,
Shifts but his place, for still the world enjoys it;
But beauty's waste hath in the world an end,
And kept unused the user so destroys it:
   No love toward others in that bosom sits
   That on himself such murd'rous shame commits.

For shame deny that thou bear'st love to any,
Who for thyself art so unprovident;
Grant, if thou wilt, thou art beloved of many,
But that thou none lov'st is most evident:
For thou art so possessed with murd'rous hate
That 'gainst thyself thou stick'st not to conspire,
Seeking that beauteous roof to ruinate
Which to repair should be thy chief desire:
O change thy thought, that I may change my mind;
Shall hate be fairer lodged than gentle love?
Be as thy presence is, gracious and kind;
Or to thyself at least kind-hearted prove,

Make thee another self for love of me,
That beauty still may live in thine or thee.

❧ II ❧

As fast as thou shalt wane, so fast thou grow'st
    In one of thine, from that which thou departest;
And that fresh blood which youngly thou bestow'st
Thou mayst call thine, when thou from youth
        convertest;
Herein lives wisdom, beauty and increase;
Without this, folly, age and cold decay.
If all were minded so, the times should cease,
And threescore year would make the world away:
Let those whom nature hath not made for store,
Harsh, featureless and rude, barrenly perish;
Look whom she best endowed, she gave the more,
Which bounteous gift thou shouldst in bounty cherish:
    She carved thee for her seal, and meant thereby
    Thou shouldst print more, not let that copy die.

WHEN I do count the clock that tells the time,
And see the brave day sunk in hideous night;
When I behold the violet past prime,
And sable curls all silvered o'er with white:
When lofty trees I see barren of leaves,
Which erst from heat did canopy the herd,
And summer's green all girded up in sheaves
Borne on the bier with white and bristly beard:
Then of thy beauty do I question make,
That thou among the wastes of time must go,
Since sweets and beauties do themselves forsake,
And die as fast as they see others grow,

   And nothing 'gainst time's scythe can make defence
   Save breed to brave him, when he takes thee hence.

O THAT you were yourself! But, love, you are
No longer yours, than you yourself here live;
Against this coming end you should prepare,
And your sweet semblance to some other give:
So should that beauty which you hold in lease
Find no determination; then you were
Yourself again after yourself's decease,
When your sweet issue your sweet form should bear.
Who lets so fair a house fall to decay,
Which husbandry in honour might uphold
Against the stormy gusts of winter's day
And barren rage of death's eternal cold?
   O none but unthrifts, dear my love you know:
   You had a father; let your son say so.

Nᴏᴛ from the stars do I my judgement pluck;
  And yet, methinks, I have astronomy,
But not to tell of good or evil luck,
Of plagues, of dearths, or seasons' quality;
Nor can I fortune to brief minutes tell,
Pointing to each his thunder, rain and wind;
Or say with princes if it shall go well
By aught predict that I in heaven find;
But from thine eyes my knowledge I derive,
And, constant stars, in them I read such art
As truth and beauty shall together thrive
If from thyself, to store thou wouldst convert:
  Or else of thee this I prognosticate,
  Thy end is truth's and beauty's doom and date.

❧ 15 ❧

WHEN I consider everything that grows
　　Holds in perfection but a little moment;
That this huge stage presenteth naught but shows
Whereon the stars in secret influence comment;
When I perceive that men as plants increase,
Cheered and checked even by the self-same sky,
Vaunt in their youthful sap, at height decrease,
And wear their brave state out of memory:
Then the conceit of this inconstant stay
Sets you, most rich in youth, before my sight,
Where wasteful time debateth with decay
To change your day of youth to sullied night:
　　And all in war with time for love of you
　　As he takes from you, I engraft you new.

❧ 16 ❧

Bᴜᴛ wherefore do not you a mightier way
Make war upon this bloody tyrant, time,
And fortify yourself in your decay
With means more blessed than my barren rhyme?
Now stand you on the top of happy hours,
And many maiden gardens, yet unset,
With virtuous wish would bear your living flowers,
Much liker than your painted counterfeit:
So should the lines of life that life repair,
Which this, time's pencil or my pupil pen,
Neither in inward worth nor outward fair,
Can make you live yourself in eyes of men:
   To give away yourself keeps yourself still,
   And you must live drawn by your own sweet skill.

❧ 17 ❧

WHO will believe my verse in time to come,
 If it were filled with your most high deserts?
Though yet, heaven knows, it is but as a tomb,
Which hides your life, and shows not half your parts:
If I could write the beauty of your eyes,
And in fresh numbers number all your graces,
The age to come would say, 'This poet lies;
Such heavenly touches ne'er touched earthly faces.'
So should my papers (yellowed with their age)
Be scorned, like old men of less truth than tongue,
And your true rights be termed a poet's rage,
And stretched metre of an antique song;
    But were some child of yours alive that time,
    You should live twice: in it, and in my rhyme.

❧ 18 ❦

SHALL I compare thee to a summer's day?
   Thou art more lovely and more temperate:
Rough winds do shake the darling buds of May,
And summer's lease hath all too short a date:
Sometime too hot the eye of heaven shines,
And often is his gold complexion dimmed;
And every fair from fair sometime declines,
By chance, or nature's changing course, untrimmed:
But thy eternal summer shall not fade,
Nor lose possession of that fair thou ow'st,
Nor shall death brag thou wander'st in his shade
When in eternal lines to time thou grow'st:
   So long as men can breathe or eyes can see,
   So long lives this, and this gives life to thee.

❧ 19 ❧

Devouring time, blunt thou the lion's paws,
  And make the earth devour her own sweet brood;
Pluck the keen teeth from the fierce tiger's jaws,
And burn the long-lived Phoenix in her blood;
Make glad and sorry seasons as thou fleet'st,
And do whate'er thou wilt, swift-footed time,
To the wide world and all her fading sweets:
But I forbid thee one most heinous crime,
O carve not with thy hours my love's fair brow,
Nor draw no lines there with thine antique pen;
Him in thy course untainted do allow
For beauty's pattern to succeeding men.
  Yet do thy worst, old Time, despite thy wrong,
  My love shall in my verse ever live young.

❧ 20 ❧

A WOMAN'S face with nature's own hand painted
   Hast thou, the master mistress of my passion;
A woman's gentle heart, but not acquainted
With shifting change, as is false women's fashion;
An eye more bright than theirs, less false in rolling,
Gilding the object whereupon it gazeth;
A man in hue, all hues in his controlling,
Which steals men's eyes and women's souls amazeth;
And for a woman wert thou first created,
Till nature as she wrought thee fell a-doting,
And by addition me of thee defeated,
By adding one thing to my purpose nothing:
   But since she pricked thee out for women's pleasure,
   Mine be thy love, and thy love's use their treasure.

So is it not with me as with that Muse,
  Stirred by a painted beauty to his verse,
Who heaven itself for ornament doth use,
And every fair with his fair doth rehearse,
Making a couplement of proud compare
With sun and moon, with earth and sea's rich gems;
With April's first-born flowers and all things rare
That heaven's air in this huge rondure hems;
O let me true in love but truly write,
And then believe me: my love is as fair
As any mother's child, though not so bright
As those gold candles fixed in heaven's air:
  Let them say more that like of hearsay well,
  I will not praise, that purpose not to sell.

❧ 22 ❧

MY glass shall not persuade me I am old
So long as youth and thou are of one date;
But when in thee time's furrows I behold,
Then look I death my days should expiate:
For all that beauty that doth cover thee
Is but the seemly raiment of my heart,
Which in thy breast doth live, as thine in me;
How can I then be elder than thou art?
O therefore love be of thyself so wary
As I not for myself, but for thee will,
Bearing thy heart, which I will keep so chary
As tender nurse her babe from faring ill:

> *Presume not on thy heart when mine is slain;*
> *Thou gav'st me thine not to give back again.*

❧ 23 ❧

As an unperfect actor on the stage,
Who with his fear is put besides his part;
Or some fierce thing, replete with too much rage,
Whose strength's abundance weakens his own heart;
So I, for fear of trust, forget to say
The perfect ceremony of love's right,
And in mine own love's strength seem to decay,
O'ercharged with burden of mine own love's might:
O let my books be then the eloquence
And dumb presagers of my speaking breast,
Who plead for love, and look for recompense,
More than that tongue that more hath more expressed:
    O learn to read what silent love hath writ!
    To hear with eyes belongs to love's fine wit.

❦ 24 ❦

M INE eye hath played the painter, and hath steeled
Thy beauty's form in table of my heart;
My body is the frame wherein 'tis held,
And perspective it is best painter's art;
For through the painter must you see his skill,
To find where your true image pictured lies,
Which in my bosom's shop is hanging still,
That hath his windows glazed with thine eyes:
Now see what good turns eyes for eyes have done:
Mine eyes have drawn thy shape, and thine for me
Are windows to my breast, wherethrough the sun
Delights to peep, to gaze therein on thee;

Yet eyes this cunning want to grace their art:
They draw but what they see, know not the heart.

L ET those who are in favour with their stars
　　Of public honour and proud titles boast,
Whilst I, whom fortune of such triumph bars,
Unlooked for joy in that I honour most;
Great princes' favourites their fair leaves spread
But as the marigold at the sun's eye,
And in themselves their pride lies buried,
For at a frown they in their glory die.
The painful warrior famoused for worth,
After a thousand victories once foiled,
Is from the book of honour razed quite,
And all the rest forgot for which he toiled:
　　Then happy I, that love and am beloved
　　Where I may not remove, nor be removed.

❧ 26 ❧

LORD of my love, to whom in vassalage
        Thy merit hath my duty strongly knit:
To thee I send this written embassage,
To witness duty, not to show my wit;
Duty so great, which wit so poor as mine
May make seem bare, in wanting words to show it;
But that I hope some good conceit of thine
In thy soul's thought (all naked) will bestow it:
Till whatsoever star that guides my moving
Points on me graciously with fair aspect,
And puts apparel on my tattered loving,
To show me worthy of thy sweet respect;

Then may I dare to boast how I do love thee;
Till then, not show my head where thou mayst
    prove me.

❧ 27 ❦

WEARY with toil, I haste me to my bed,
   The dear repose for limbs with travail tired;
But then begins a journey in my head
To work my mind, when body's work's expired:
For then my thoughts, from far where I abide,
Intend a zealous pilgrimage to thee,
And keep my drooping eyelids open wide,
Looking on darkness which the blind do see;
Save that my soul's imaginary sight
Presents thy shadow to my sightless view,
Which like a jewel hung in ghastly night
Makes black night beauteous, and her old face new:
   Lo, thus by day my limbs, by night my mind,
   For thee, and for myself, no quiet find.

How can I then return in happy plight
That am debarred the benefit of rest?
When day's oppression is not eased by night,
But day by night and night by day oppressed,
And each, though enemies to either's reign,
Do in consent shake hands to torture me,
The one by toil, the other to complain
How far I toil, still farther off from thee.
I tell the day to please him, thou art bright,
And dost him grace, when clouds do blot the heaven;
So flatter I the swart-complexioned night,
When sparkling stars twire not thou gild'st the even;

But day doth daily draw my sorrows longer,
And night doth nightly make grief's length seem
stronger.

❧ 29 ❧

WHEN in disgrace with fortune and men's eyes
I all alone beweep my outcast state,
And trouble deaf heav'n with my bootless cries,
And look upon myself, and curse my fate,
Wishing me like to one more rich in hope,
Featured like him, like him with friends possessed,
Desiring this man's art and that man's scope,
With what I most enjoy contented least;
Yet in these thoughts myself almost despising,
Haply I think on thee, and then my state,
Like to the lark at break of day arising,
From sullen earth sings hymns at heaven's gate;

For thy sweet love remembered such wealth brings
That then I scorn to change my state with kings.

WHEN to the sessions of sweet silent thought
    I summon up remembrance of things past,
I sigh the lack of many a thing I sought,
And with old woes new wail my dear time's waste;
Then can I drown an eye (unused to flow)
For precious friends hid in death's dateless night,
And weep afresh love's long since cancelled woe,
And moan th'expense of many a vanished sight.
Then can I grieve at grievances foregone,
And heavily from woe to woe tell o'er
The sad account of fore-bemoaned moan,
Which I new pay, as if not paid before;
    But if the while I think on thee, dear friend,
    All losses are restored, and sorrows end.

THY bosom is endeared with all hearts
    Which I, by lacking, have supposed dead;
And there reigns love, and all love's loving parts,
And all those friends which I thought buried.
How many a holy and obsequious tear
Hath dear religious love stol'n from mine eye,
As interest of the dead, which now appear
But things removed that hidden in thee lie:
Thou art the grave where buried love doth live,
Hung with the trophies of my lovers gone,
Who all their parts of me to thee did give;
That due of many, now is thine alone.
    Their images I loved, I view in thee,
    And thou, all they, hast all the all of me.

IF thou survive my well-contented day,
  When that churl death my bones with dust shall
    cover,
And shalt by fortune once more re-survey
These poor rude lines of thy deceased lover:
Compare them with the bett'ring of the time,
And though they be outstripped by every pen,
Reserve them for my love, not for their rhyme,
Exceeded by the height of happier men.
O then vouchsafe me but this loving thought:
'Had my friend's Muse grown with this growing age,
A dearer birth than this his love had brought,
To march in ranks of better equipage:
    But since he died and poets better prove,
    Theirs for their style I'll read, his for his love.'

FULL many a glorious morning have I seen
   Flatter the mountain tops with sovereign eye,
Kissing with golden face the meadows green,
Gilding pale streams with heavenly alchemy;
Anon permit the basest clouds to ride
With ugly rack on his celestial face,
And from the forlorn world his visage hide,
Stealing unseen to west with this disgrace:
Even so my sun one early morn did shine
With all triumphant splendour on my brow;
But out alack, he was but one hour mine,
The region cloud hath masked him from me now.
   Yet him for this, my love no whit disdaineth:
   Suns of the world may stain, when heaven's sun
      staineth.

❧ 34 ❧

WHY didst thou promise such a beauteous day
     And make me travail forth without my cloak,
To let base clouds o'ertake me in my way,
Hiding thy brav'ry in their rotten smoke?
'Tis not enough that through the cloud thou break,
To dry the rain on my storm-beaten face,
For no man well of such a salve can speak
That heals the wound and cures not the disgrace;
Nor can thy shame give physic to my grief;
Though thou repent, yet I have still the loss;
Th'offender's sorrow lends but weak relief
To him that bears the strong offence's loss.
　　Ah, but those tears are pearl which thy love sheds,
　　And they are rich, and ransom all ill deeds.

🦋 35 🦋

No more be grieved at that which thou hast done;
Roses have thorns, and silver fountains mud;
Clouds and eclipses stain both moon and sun,
And loathsome canker lives in sweetest bud.
All men make faults, and even I, in this,
Authorizing thy trespass with compare,
Myself corrupting, salving thy amiss,
Excusing these sins more than these sins are:
For to thy sensual fault I bring in sense;
Thy adverse party is thy advocate,
And 'gainst myself a lawful plea commence:
Such civil war is in my love and hate
    That I an accessory needs must be
    To that sweet thief which sourly robs from me.

❧ 36 ❧

LET me confess that we two must be twain,
  Although our undivided loves are one;
So shall those blots that do with me remain,
Without thy help, by me be borne alone.
In our two loves there is but one respect,
Though in our lives a separable spite;
Which, though it alter not love's sole effect,
Yet doth it steal sweet hours from love's delight.
I may not evermore acknowledge thee,
Lest my bewailed guilt should do thee shame,
Nor thou with public kindness honour me,
Unless thou take that honour from thy name:
  But do not so; I love thee in such sort,
  As thou being mine, mine is thy good report.

As a decrepit father takes delight
    To see his active child do deeds of youth,
So I, made lame by fortune's dearest spite,
Take all my comfort of thy worth and truth:
For whether beauty, birth, or wealth, or wit,
Or any of these all, or all, or more,
Entitled in thy parts do crowned sit,
I make my love engrafted to this store:
So then I am not lame, poor, nor despised,
Whilst that this shadow doth such substance give
That I in thy abundance am sufficed,
And by a part of all thy glory live:
    Look what is best, that best I wish in thee;
    This wish I have, then ten times happy me.

❧ 38 ❧

How can my Muse want subject to invent
 While thou dost breathe, that pour'st into
  my verse
Thine own sweet argument, too excellent
For every vulgar paper to rehearse?
O give thyself the thanks, if aught in me
Worthy perusal stand against thy sight:
For who's so dumb, that cannot write to thee,
When thou thyself dost give invention light?
Be thou the tenth Muse, ten times more in worth
Than those old nine which rhymers invocate;
And he that calls on thee, let him bring forth
Eternal numbers to outlive long date.

 If my slight Muse do please these curious days,
  The pain be mine, but thine shall be the praise.

❦ 39 ❧

O HOW thy worth with manners may I sing,
　　When thou art all the better part of me?
What can mine own praise to mine own self bring,
And what is't but mine own, when I praise thee?
Even for this, let us divided live,
And our dear love lose name of single one,
That by this separation I may give
That due to thee which thou deserv'st alone.
O absence, what a torment wouldst thou prove,
Were it not thy sour leisure gave sweet leave
To entertain the time with thoughts of love,
Which time and thoughts so sweetly dost deceive,
　　And that thou teachest how to make one twain
　　By praising him here who doth hence remain.

Take all my loves, my love; yea, take them all;
What hast thou then more than thou hadst before?
No love, my love, that thou mayst true love call;
All mine was thine, before thou hadst this more:
Then if for my love thou my love receivest,
I cannot blame thee, for my love thou usest;
But yet be blamed, if thou thyself deceivest
By wilful taste of what thyself refusest.
I do forgive thy robb'ry, gentle thief,
Although thou steal thee all my poverty;
And yet love knows it is a greater grief
To bear love's wrong, than hate's known injury.

Lascivious grace, in whom all ill well shows,
Kill me with spites; yet we must not be foes.

THOSE pretty wrongs that liberty commits
   When I am sometime absent from thy heart,
Thy beauty and thy years full well befits;
For still temptation follows where thou art.
Gentle thou art, and therefore to be won;
Beauteous thou art, therefore to be assailed;
And when a woman woos, what woman's son
Will sourly leave her till he have prevailed?
Ay me, but yet thou mightst my seat forbear,
And chide thy beauty and thy straying youth
Who lead thee in their riot even there
Where thou art forced to break a twofold truth:
   Hers by thy beauty tempting her to thee,
   Thine by thy beauty being false to me.

THAT thou hast her it is not all my grief,
  And yet it may be said I loved her dearly;
That she hath thee is of my wailing chief,
A loss in love that touches me more nearly.
Loving offenders, thus I will excuse ye:
Thou dost love her, because thou knowst I love her,
And for my sake even so doth she abuse me,
Suff'ring my friend for my sake to approve her;
If I lose thee, my loss is my love's gain,
And losing her, my friend hath found that loss;
Both find each other, and I lose both twain,
And both for my sake lay on me this cross:
  But here's the joy, my friend and I are one;
  Sweet flattery! Then she loves but me alone.

❧ 43 ❧

WHEN most I wink, then do mine eyes best see;
　　For all the day they view things unrespected,
But when I sleep, in dreams they look on thee,
And darkly bright, are bright in dark directed.
Then thou whose shadow shadows doth make bright,
How would thy shadow's form form happy show
To the clear day with thy much clearer light,
When to unseeing eyes thy shade shines so?
How would (I say) mine eyes be blessed made
By looking on thee in the living day,
When in dead night thy fair imperfect shade
Through heavy sleep on sightless eyes doth stay?
　　All days are nights to see till I see thee,
　　And nights bright days when dreams do show thee me.

44

IF the dull substance of my flesh were thought,
Injurious distance should not stop my way;
For then, despite of space, I would be brought
From limits far remote, where thou dost stay;
No matter then although my foot did stand
Upon the farthest earth removed from thee,
For nimble thought can jump both sea and land
As soon as think the place where he would be.
But ah, thought kills me, that I am not thought,
To leap large lengths of miles when thou art gone,
But that so much of earth and water wrought,
I must attend time's leisure with my moan;
    Receiving naughts by elements so slow
    But heavy tears, badges of either's woe.

𝕰 45 𝕰

THE other two, slight air, and purging fire,
  Are both with thee, wherever I abide:
The first my thought, the other my desire,
These, present absent, with swift motion slide;
For when these quicker elements are gone
In tender embassy of love to thee,
My life being made of four, with two alone
Sinks down to death, oppressed with melancholy,
Until life's composition be recured
By those swift messengers returned from thee
Who even but now come back again assured
Of thy fair health, recounting it to me.
  This told, I joy; but then no longer glad,
  I send them back again and straight grow sad.

MINE eye and heart are at a mortal war
    How to divide the conquest of thy sight;
Mine eye, my heart thy picture's sight would bar;
My heart, mine eye the freedom of that right;
My heart doth plead that thou in him dost lie,
A closet never pierced with crystal eyes;
But the defendant doth that plea deny,
And says in him thy fair appearance lies.
To find this title is empanelled
A quest of thoughts, all tenants to the heart,
And by their verdict is determined
The clear eyes' moiety, and the dear heart's part:
    As thus, mine eyes' due is thy outward part,
    And my heart's right, thy inward love of heart.

Betwixt mine eye and heart a league is took,
And each doth good turns now unto the other;
When that mine eye is famished for a look,
Or heart in love with sighs himself doth smother,
With my love's picture then my eye doth feast,
And to the painted banquet bids my heart;
Another time mine eye is my heart's guest,
And in his thoughts of love doth share a part.
So either by thy picture or my love,
Thyself away, art present still with me:
For thou no further than my thoughts canst move,
And I am still with them, and they with thee;
   Or if they sleep, thy picture in my sight
   Awakes my heart to heart's and eye's delight.

❧ 48 ❧

How careful was I, when I took my way,
Each trifle under truest bars to thrust,
That to my use it might unused stay
From hands of falsehood, in sure wards of trust;
But thou, to whom my jewels trifles are,
Most worthy comfort, now my greatest grief,
Thou best of dearest, and mine only care,
Art left the prey of every vulgar thief.
Thee have I not locked up in any chest,
Save where thou art not, though I feel thou art,
Within the gentle closure of my breast,
From whence at pleasure thou mayst come and part;
    And even thence thou wilt be stol'n, I fear;
    For truth proves thievish for a prize so dear.

AGAINST that time, if ever that time come,
  When I shall see thee frown on my defects;
Whenas thy love hath cast his utmost sum,
Called to that audit by advised respects;
Against that time when thou shalt strangely pass,
And scarcely greet me with that sun, thine eye;
When love, converted from the thing it was,
Shall reasons find of settled gravity;
Against that time do I ensconce me here,
Within the knowledge of mine own desert,
And this my hand against myself uprear,
To guard the lawful reasons on thy part:

To leave poor me, thou hast the strength of laws,
Since why to love, I can allege no cause.

❧ 50 ❧

How heavy do I journey on the way
    When what I seek, my weary travel's end,
Doth teach that ease and that repose to say,
'Thus far the miles are measured from thy friend.'
The beast that bears me, tired with my woe,
Plods dully on to bear that weight in me,
As if by some instinct the wretch did know
His rider loved not speed being made from thee:
The bloody spur cannot provoke him on
That sometimes anger thrusts into his hide,
Which heavily he answers with a groan,
More sharp to me than spurring to his side,

    For that same groan doth put this in my mind:
    My grief lies onward and my joy behind.

THUS can my love excuse the slow offence
  Of my dull bearer, when from thee I speed:
From where thou art, why should I haste me thence?
Till I return, of posting is no need.
O what excuse will my poor beast then find,
When swift extremity can seem but slow?
Then should I spur, though mounted on the wind;
In winged speed no motion shall I know;
Then can no horse with my desire keep pace;
Therefore desire, of perfect'st love being made,
Shall neigh no dull flesh in his fiery race,
But love, for love, thus shall excuse my jade:
    Since from thee going he went wilful slow,
    Towards thee I'll run, and give him leave to go.

So am I as the rich, whose blessed key
  Can bring him to his sweet up-locked treasure,
The which he will not every hour survey,
For blunting the fine point of seldom pleasure;
Therefore are feasts so solemn and so rare,
Since, seldom coming, in the long year set,
Like stones of worth they thinly placed are,
Or captain jewels in the carcanet.
So is the time that keeps you as my chest,
Or as the wardrobe which the robe doth hide,
To make some special instant special blessed
By new unfolding his imprisoned pride.
  Blessed are you, whose worthiness gives scope,
  Being had, to triumph; being lacked, to hope.

WHAT is your substance, whereof are you made,
That millions of strange shadows on you tend?
Since every one hath every one one shade,
And you, but one, can every shadow lend;
Describe Adonis, and the counterfeit
Is poorly imitated after you;
On Helen's cheek all art of beauty set
And you in Grecian tires are painted new;
Speak of the spring, and foison of the year:
The one doth shadow of your beauty show,
The other as your bounty doth appear,
And you in every blessed shape we know.

In all external grace you have some part,
But you like none, none you, for constant heart.

54

O HOW much more doth beauty beauteous seem
By that sweet ornament which truth doth give!
The rose looks fair, but fairer we it deem
For that sweet odour which doth in it live;
The canker blooms have full as deep a dye
As the perfumed tincture of the roses,
Hang on such thorns, and play as wantonly,
When summer's breath their masked buds discloses;
But for their virtue only is their show
They live unwooed, and unrespected fade,
Die to themselves. Sweet roses do not so;
Of their sweet deaths are sweetest odours made;
  And so of you, beauteous and lovely youth;
  When that shall vade, by verse distils your truth.

Not marble, nor the gilded monuments
    Of princes, shall outlive this powerful rhyme;
But you shall shine more bright in these contents
Than unswept stone, besmeared with sluttish time.
When wasteful war shall statues overturn
And broils root out the work of masonry,
Nor Mars his sword, nor war's quick fire, shall burn
The living record of your memory:
'Gainst death, and all oblivious enmity,
Shall you pace forth; your praise shall still find room
Even in the eyes of all posterity
That wear this world out to the ending doom.
    So till the judgement that yourself arise,
    You live in this, and dwell in lovers' eyes.

S WEET love, renew thy force; be it not said
Thy edge should blunter be than appetite,
Which but today by feeding is allayed,
Tomorrow sharpened in his former might;
So, love, be thou; although today thou fill
Thy hungry eyes even till they wink with fullness,
Tomorrow see again, and do not kill
The spirit of love with a perpetual dullness;
Let this sad interim like the ocean be
Which parts the shore, where two contracted new
Come daily to the banks, that when they see
Return of love, more blessed may be the view;

Or call it winter, which being full of care
Makes summer's welcome thrice more wished, more
rare.

Being your slave, what should I do but tend
Upon the hours and times of your desire?
I have no precious time at all to spend,
Nor services to do, till you require;
Nor dare I chide the world-without-end hour
Whilst I, my sovereign, watch the clock for you,
Nor think the bitterness of absence sour
When you have bid your servant once adieu;
Nor dare I question with my jealous thought
Where you may be, or your affairs suppose,
But like a sad slave stay and think of naught,
Save, where you are, how happy you make those.
    So true a fool is love, that in your will,
    Though you do anything, he thinks no ill.

💥 58 🦋

THAT god forbid, that made me first your slave,
I should in thought control your times of pleasure,
Or at your hand th'account of hours to crave,
Being your vassal bound to stay your leisure.
O let me suffer, being at your beck,
Th'imprisoned absence of your liberty,
And patience tame, to sufferance bide each check,
Without accusing you of injury.
Be where you list, your charter is so strong
That you yourself may privilege your time
To what you will; to you it doth belong
Yourself to pardon of self-doing crime.

I am to wait, though waiting so be hell,
Not blame your pleasure be it ill or well.

IF there be nothing new, but that which is
  Hath been before, how are our brains beguiled,
Which, labouring for invention, bear amiss
The second burden of a former child?
O that record could with a backward look
Even of five hundred courses of the sun
Show me your image in some antique book,
Since mind at first in character was done,
That I might see what the old world could say
To this composed wonder of your frame;
Whether we are mended, or whe'er better they,
Or whether revolution be the same.
   O sure I am, the wits of former days
   To subjects worse have given admiring praise.

Like as the waves make towards the pebbled shore,
So do our minutes hasten to their end,
Each changing place with that which goes before,
In sequent toil all forwards do contend.
Nativity, once in the main of light,
Crawls to maturity; wherewith being crowned
Crooked eclipses 'gainst his glory fight,
And time, that gave, doth now his gift confound.
Time doth transfix the flourish set on youth,
And delves the parallels in beauty's brow;
Feeds on the rarities of nature's truth,
And nothing stands but for his scythe to mow.
   And yet to times in hope my verse shall stand,
   Praising thy worth, despite his cruel hand.

❧ 61 ❧

Is it thy will thy image should keep open
My heavy eyelids to the weary night?
Dost thou desire my slumbers should be broken
While shadows like to thee do mock my sight?
Is it thy spirit that thou send'st from thee
So far from home into my deeds to pry,
To find out shames and idle hours in me,
The scope and tenor of thy jealousy?
O no, thy love, though much, is not so great;
It is my love that keeps mine eye awake,
Mine own true love that doth my rest defeat,
To play the watchman ever for thy sake.
　　For thee watch I, whilst thou dost wake elsewhere,
　　From me far off, with others all too near.

Sin of self-love possesseth all mine eye,
And all my soul, and all my every part;
And for this sin there is no remedy,
It is so grounded inward in my heart.
Methinks no face so gracious is as mine,
No shape so true, no truth of such account,
And for myself mine own worth do define
As I all other in all worths surmount.
But when my glass shows me myself indeed,
Beated and chopped with tanned antiquity,
Mine own self-love quite contrary I read;
Self, so self-loving, were iniquity;

   'Tis thee (myself) that for myself I praise,
   Painting my age with beauty of thy days.

❧ 63 ❧

AGAINST my love shall be as I am now,
 With time's injurious hand crushed and o'erworn;
When hours have drained his blood, and filled his brow
With lines and wrinkles; when his youthful morn
Hath travailed on to age's steepy night,
And all those beauties whereof now he's king
Are vanishing, or vanished out of sight,
Stealing away the treasure of his spring;
For such a time do I now fortify
Against confounding age's cruel knife,
That he shall never cut from memory
My sweet love's beauty, though my lover's life.
  His beauty shall in these black lines be seen,
  And they shall live, and he in them still green.

❧ 64 ❧

WHEN I have seen by time's fell hand defaced
  The rich proud cost of outworn buried age;
When sometime lofty towers I see down razed,
And brass eternal slave to mortal rage;
When I have seen the hungry ocean gain
Advantage on the kingdom of the shore,
And the firm soil win of the wat'ry main,
Increasing store with loss, and loss with store;
When I have seen such interchange of state,
Or state itself confounded, to decay,
Ruin hath taught me thus to ruminate:
That time will come and take my love away.
  This thought is as a death, which cannot choose
  But weep to have that which it fears to lose.

❧ 65 ❧

SINCE brass, nor stone, nor earth, nor boundless sea,
But sad mortality o'er-sways their power,
How with this rage shall beauty hold a plea,
Whose action is no stronger than a flower?
O how shall summer's honey breath hold out
Against the wrackful siege of batt'ring days
When rocks impregnable are not so stout,
Nor gates of steel so strong, but time decays?
O fearful meditation! Where, alack,
Shall time's best jewel from time's chest lie hid?
Or what strong hand can hold his swift foot back,
Or who his spoil o'er beauty can forbid?
   O none, unless this miracle have might:
   That in black ink my love may still shine bright.

❧ 66 ❧

TIRED with all these for restful death I cry:
As to behold desert a beggar born,
And needy nothing trimmed in jollity,
And purest faith unhappily forsworn,
And gilded honour shamefully misplaced,
And maiden virtue rudely strumpeted,
And right perfection wrongfully disgraced,
And strength by limping sway disabled,
And art made tongue-tied by authority,
And folly, doctor-like, controlling skill,
And simple truth miscalled simplicity,
And captive good attending captain ill:
    Tired with all these, from these would I be gone,
    Save that to die I leave my love alone.

Ah, wherefore with infection should he live,
    And with his presence grace impiety,
That sin by him advantage should achieve,
And lace itself with his society?
Why should false painting imitate his cheek,
And steal dead seeing of his living hue?
Why should poor beauty indirectly seek
Roses of shadow, since his rose is true?
Why should he live, now nature bankrupt is,
Beggared of blood to blush through lively veins?
For she hath no exchequer now but his,
And proud of many, lives upon his gains.
    O, him she stores, to show what wealth she had
    In days long since, before these last so bad.

❦ 68 ❦

Thus is his cheek the map of days outworn,
   When beauty lived and died as flowers do now,
Before these bastard signs of fair were borne,
Or durst inhabit on a living brow;
Before the golden tresses of the dead,
The right of sepulchres, were shorn away,
To live a second life on second head;
Ere beauty's dead fleece made another gay:
In him those holy antique hours are seen,
Without all ornament, itself and true,
Making no summer of another's green,
Robbing no old to dress his beauty new;
   And him as for a map doth nature store
   To show false art what beauty was of yore.

✖ 69 ✖

THOSE parts of thee that the world's eye doth view
   Want nothing that the thought of hearts can mend;
All tongues, the voice of souls, give thee that due,
Utt'ring bare truth, even so as foes commend:
Thy outward thus with outward praise is crowned.
But those same tongues that give thee so thine own
In other accents do this praise confound,
By seeing further than the eye hath shown;
They look into the beauty of thy mind,
And that in guess they measure by thy deeds;
Then churls their thoughts (although their eyes were
      kind)
To thy fair flower add the rank smell of weeds.
   But why thy odour matcheth not thy show,
   The soil is this, that thou dost common grow.

THAT thou art blamed shall not be thy defect,
For slander's mark was ever yet the fair;
The ornament of beauty is suspect,
A crow that flies in heaven's sweetest air.
So thou be good, slander doth but approve
Thy worth the greater, being wooed of time;
For canker vice the sweetest buds doth love,
And thou present'st a pure unstained prime.
Thou hast passed by the ambush of young days,
Either not assailed, or victor, being charged;
Yet this thy praise cannot be so thy praise,
To tie up envy, evermore enlarged:

If some suspect of ill masked not thy show
Then thou alone kingdoms of hearts shouldst owe.

No longer mourn for me when I am dead
Than you shall hear the surly sullen bell
Give warning to the world that I am fled
From this vile world, with vilest worms to dwell:
Nay, if you read this line, remember not
The hand that writ it, for I love you so
That I in your sweet thoughts would be forgot,
If thinking on me then should make you woe.
O if (I say) you look upon this verse,
When I, perhaps, compounded am with clay,
Do not so much as my poor name rehearse,
But let your love even with my life decay;
   Lest the wise world should look into your moan,
   And mock you with me after I am gone.

O LEST the world should task you to recite
　　What merit lived in me that you should love,
After my death (dear love) forget me quite,
For you in me can nothing worthy prove;
Unless you would devise some virtuous lie
To do more for me than mine own desert,
And hang more praise upon deceased I
Than niggard truth would willingly impart;
O, lest your true love may seem false in this,
That you for love speak well of me untrue,
My name be buried where my body is,
And live no more to shame nor me, nor you:

　　For I am shamed by that which I bring forth,
　　And so should you, to love things nothing worth.

THAT time of year thou mayst in me behold,
When yellow leaves, or none, or few do hang
Upon those boughs which shake against the cold,
Bare ruined choirs where late the sweet birds sang;
In me thou seest the twilight of such day
As after sunset fadeth in the west,
Which by and by black night doth take away,
Death's second self that seals up all in rest;
In me thou seest the glowing of such fire
That on the ashes of his youth doth lie,
As the deathbed, whereon it must expire,
Consumed with that which it was nourished by;

This thou perceiv'st, which makes thy love more strong,
To love that well, which thou must leave ere long.

❧ 74 ❧

B<small>UT</small> be contented when that fell arrest
Without all bail shall carry me away;
My life hath in this line some interest,
Which for memorial still with thee shall stay.
When thou reviewest this, thou dost review
The very part was consecrate to thee;
The earth can have but earth, which is his due,
My spirit is thine, the better part of me;
So then thou hast but lost the dregs of life,
The prey of worms, my body being dead,
The coward conquest of a wretch's knife,
Too base of thee to be remembered:

The worth of that, is that which it contains,
And that is this, and this with thee remains.

So are you to my thoughts as food to life,
 Or as sweet seasoned showers to the ground;
And for the peace of you I hold such strife
As 'twixt a miser and his wealth is found:
Now proud as an enjoyer, and anon
Doubting the filching age will steal his treasure;
Now counting best to be with you alone,
Then bettered that the world may see my pleasure;
Sometime all full with feasting on your sight,
And by and by clean starved for a look,
Possessing or pursuing no delight
Save what is had, or must from you be took.
 Thus do I pine and surfeit day by day,
 Or gluttoning on all, or all away.

WHY is my verse so barren of new pride,
So far from variation or quick change?
Why with the time do I not glance aside
To new-found methods and to compounds strange?
Why write I still all one, ever the same,
And keep invention in a noted weed,
That every word doth almost tell my name,
Showing their birth, and where they did proceed?
O know, sweet love, I always write of you,
And you and love are still my argument:
So all my best is dressing old words new,
Spending again what is already spent:

   For as the sun is daily new and old,
   So is my love still telling what is told.

THY glass will show thee how thy beauties wear,
Thy dial how thy precious minutes waste,
The vacant leaves thy mind's imprint will bear,
And of this book, this learning mayst thou taste:
The wrinkles which thy glass will truly show
Of mouthed graves will give thee memory;
Thou by thy dial's shady stealth mayst know
Time's thievish progress to eternity;
Look what thy memory cannot contain,
Commit to these waste blanks, and thou shalt find
Those children nursed, delivered from thy brain,
To take a new acquaintance of thy mind.
 These offices, so oft as thou wilt look,
 Shall profit thee, and much enrich thy book.

So oft have I invoked thee for my Muse,
 And found such fair assistance in my verse,
As every alien pen hath got my use,
And under thee their poesy disperse.
Thine eyes, that taught the dumb on high to sing,
And heavy ignorance aloft to fly,
Have added feathers to the learned's wing,
And given grace a double majesty.
Yet be most proud of that which I compile,
Whose influence is thine, and born of thee:
In others' works thou dost but mend the style,
And arts with thy sweet graces graced be;
    But thou art all my art, and dost advance,
    As high as learning, my rude ignorance.

WHILST I alone did call upon thy aid
　　My verse alone had all thy gentle grace;
But now my gracious numbers are decayed,
And my sick Muse doth give another place.
I grant, sweet love, thy lovely argument
Deserves the travail of a worthier pen;
Yet what of thee thy poet doth invent
He robs thee of, and pays it thee again;
He lends thee virtue, and he stole that word
From thy behaviour; beauty doth he give,
And found it in thy cheek; he can afford
No praise to thee, but what in thee doth live:

    Then thank him not for that which he doth say,
    Since what he owes thee, thou thyself dost pay.

O HOW I faint when I of you do write,
　　Knowing a better spirit doth use your name,
And in the praise thereof spends all his might,
To make me tongue-tied speaking of your fame.
But since your worth, wide as the ocean is,
The humble as the proudest sail doth bear,
My saucy bark, inferior far to his,
On your broad main doth wilfully appear.
Your shallowest help will hold me up afloat,
Whilst he upon your soundless deep doth ride;
Or, being wracked, I am a worthless boat,
He of tall building, and of goodly pride.
　　Then if he thrive, and I be cast away,
　　The worst was this: my love was my decay.

Or I shall live, your epitaph to make;
Or you survive, when I in earth am rotten;
From hence your memory death cannot take,
Although in me each part will be forgotten.
Your name from hence immortal life shall have,
Though I, once gone, to all the world must die;
The earth can yield me but a common grave,
When you entombed in men's eyes shall lie.
Your monument shall be my gentle verse,
Which eyes not yet created shall o'er-read,
And tongues to be your being shall rehearse,
When all the breathers of this world are dead.
You still shall live, such virtue hath my pen,
Where breath most breathes, even in the mouths
of men.

I GRANT thou wert not married to my Muse,
  And therefore mayst without attaint o'erlook
The dedicated words which writers use
Of their fair subject, blessing every book.
Thou art as fair in knowledge as in hue,
Finding thy worth a limit past my praise,
And therefore art enforced to seek anew
Some fresher stamp of the time-bettering days,
And do so love; yet when they have devised
What strained touches rhetoric can lend,
Thou, truly fair, wert truly sympathized
In true plain words, by thy true-telling friend;

> *And their gross painting might be better used*
> *Where cheeks need blood; in thee it is abused.*

❧ 83 ❧

I NEVER saw that you did painting need,
   And therefore to your fair no painting set;
I found (or thought I found) you did exceed
The barren tender of a poet's debt;
And therefore have I slept in your report,
That you yourself, being extant, well might show
How far a modern quill doth come too short,
Speaking of worth, what worth in you doth grow.
This silence for my sin you did impute,
Which shall be most my glory, being dumb;
For I impair not beauty, being mute,
When others would give life, and bring a tomb.
   There lives more life in one of your fair eyes
   Than both your poets can in praise devise.

❦ 84 ❦

WHO is it that says most? Which can say more,
   Than this rich praise: that you alone are you,
In whose confine immured is the store
Which should example where your equal grew?
Lean penury within that pen doth dwell
That to his subject lends not some small glory;
But he that writes of you, if he can tell
That you are you, so dignifies his story.
Let him but copy what in you is writ,
Not making worse what nature made so clear,
And such a counterpart shall fame his wit,
Making his style admired everywhere.
   You to your beauteous blessings add a curse,
   Being fond on praise, which makes your praises worse.

❧ 85 ❧

M Y tongue-tied Muse in manners holds her still,
  While comments of your praise richly compiled
Reserve your character with golden quill,
And precious phrase by all the Muses filed;
I think good thoughts, whilst other write good words,
And like unlettered clerk still cry 'Amen'
To every hymn that able spirit affords
In polished form of well-refined pen.
Hearing you praised, I say, ''Tis so, 'tis true',
And to the most of praise add something more;
But that is in my thought, whose love to you
(Though words come hindmost) holds his rank before;
  Then others for the breath of words respect,
  Me for my dumb thoughts, speaking in effect.

❧ 86 ❧

WAS it the proud full sail of his great verse,
　　Bound for the prize of all-too-precious you,
That did my ripe thoughts in my brain in-hearse,
Making their tomb the womb wherein they grew?
Was it his spirit, by spirits taught to write
Above a mortal pitch, that struck me dead?
No, neither he, nor his compeers by night,
Giving him aid, my verse astonished.
He, nor that affable familiar ghost
Which nightly gulls him with intelligence,
As victors of my silence cannot boast;
I was not sick of any fear from thence.

　　But when your countenance filled up his line,
　　Then lacked I matter, that enfeebled mine.

✻ 87 ✻

FAREWELL, thou art too dear for my possessing,
And like enough thou knowst thy estimate;
The charter of thy worth gives thee releasing;
My bonds in thee are all determinate.
For how do I hold thee but by thy granting,
And for that riches where is my deserving?
The cause of this fair gift in me is wanting,
And so my patent back again is swerving.
Thyself thou gav'st, thy own worth then not knowing,
Or me, to whom thou gav'st it, else mistaking;
So thy great gift upon misprision growing
Comes home again, on better judgement making.
  Thus have I had thee as a dream doth flatter,
  In sleep a king, but waking no such matter.

WHEN thou shalt be disposed to set me light
　　And place my merit in the eye of scorn,
Upon thy side, against myself, I'll fight,
And prove thee virtuous, though thou art forsworn:
With mine own weakness being best acquainted,
Upon thy part I can set down a story
Of faults concealed, wherein I am attainted,
That thou, in losing me, shall win much glory;
And I by this will be a gainer too,
For bending all my loving thoughts on thee,
The injuries that to myself I do,
Doing thee vantage, double vantage me:

 Such is my love, to thee I so belong,
 That for thy right myself will bear all wrong.

❧ 89 ❧

Say that thou didst forsake me for some fault,
  And I will comment upon that offence;
Speak of my lameness, and I straight will halt,
Against thy reasons making no defence.
Thou canst not, love, disgrace me half so ill,
To set a form upon desired change,
As I'll myself disgrace, knowing thy will;
I will acquaintance strangle and look strange,
Be absent from thy walks, and in my tongue
Thy sweet beloved name no more shall dwell,
Lest I, too much profane, should do it wrong,
And haply of our old acquaintance tell.
  For thee, against myself I'll vow debate;
  For I must ne'er love him whom thou dost hate.

THEN hate me when thou wilt, if ever, now,
  Now, while the world is bent my deeds to cross,
Join with the spite of fortune, make me bow,
And do not drop in for an after-loss.
Ah, do not, when my heart hath 'scaped this sorrow,
Come in the rearward of a conquered woe;
Give not a windy night a rainy morrow,
To linger out a purposed overthrow.
If thou wilt leave me, do not leave me last,
When other petty griefs have done their spite;
But in the onset come, so shall I taste
At first the very worst of fortune's might;
  And other strains of woe, which now seem woe,
  Compared with loss of thee, will not seem so.

Some glory in their birth, some in their skill,
  Some in their wealth, some in their bodies' force,
Some in their garments, though new-fangled ill,
Some in their hawks and hounds, some in their horse,
And every humour hath his adjunct pleasure,
Wherein it finds a joy above the rest;
But these particulars are not my measure;
All these I better in one general best.
Thy love is better than high birth to me,
Richer than wealth, prouder than garments' cost,
Of more delight than hawks or horses be;
And having thee, of all men's pride I boast —
  Wretched in this alone, that thou mayst take
  All this away, and me most wretched make.

B UT do thy worst to steal thyself away;
For term of life thou art assured mine,
And life no longer than thy love will stay,
For it depends upon that love of thine.
Then need I not to fear the worst of wrongs,
When in the least of them my life hath end;
I see a better state to me belongs
Than that which on thy humour doth depend.
Thou canst not vex me with inconstant mind,
Since that my life on thy revolt doth lie.
O what a happy title do I find,
Happy to have thy love, happy to die!

   But what's so blessed fair that fears no blot?
   Thou mayst be false, and yet I know it not.

❧ 93 ❧

So shall I live, supposing thou art true,
  Like a deceived husband; so love's face
May still seem love to me, though altered new,
Thy looks with me, thy heart in other place;
For there can live no hatred in thine eye,
Therefore in that I cannot know thy change.
In many's looks, the false heart's history
Is writ in moods and frowns and wrinkles strange;
But heaven in thy creation did decree
That in thy face sweet love should ever dwell;
Whate'er thy thoughts or thy heart's workings be,
Thy looks should nothing thence but sweetness tell.
  How like Eve's apple doth thy beauty grow,
  If thy sweet virtue answer not thy show.

THEY that have power to hurt, and will do none,
  That do not do the thing they most do show,
Who, moving others, are themselves as stone,
Unmoved, cold, and to temptation slow:
They rightly do inherit heaven's graces,
And husband nature's riches from expense;
They are the lords and owners of their faces,
Others, but stewards of their excellence.
The summer's flower is to the summer sweet,
Though to itself it only live and die,
But if that flower with base infection meet,
The basest weed outbraves his dignity:
  For sweetest things turn sourest by their deeds;
  Lilies that fester smell far worse than weeds.

How sweet and lovely dost thou make the shame
  Which like a canker in the fragrant rose
Doth spot the beauty of thy budding name:
O in what sweets dost thou thy sins enclose!
That tongue that tells the story of thy days,
Making lascivious comments on thy sport,
Cannot dispraise; but in a kind of praise,
Naming thy name, blesses an ill report.
O what a mansion have those vices got,
Which for their habitation chose out thee,
Where beauty's veil doth cover every blot,
And all things turns to fair that eyes can see!
  Take heed, dear heart, of this large privilege;
  The hardest knife ill used doth lose his edge.

SOME say thy fault is youth, some wantonness;
    Some say thy grace is youth and gentle sport;
Both grace and faults are loved of more and less;
Thou mak'st faults graces, that to thee resort:
As on the finger of a throned queen
The basest jewel will be well esteemed,
So are those errors that in thee are seen
To truths translated, and for true things deemed.
How many lambs might the stern wolf betray
If like a lamb he could his looks translate?
How many gazers mightst thou lead away
If thou wouldst use the strength of all thy state?
    But do not so; I love thee in such sort,
    As thou being mine, mine is thy good report.

How like a winter hath my absence been
From thee, the pleasure of the fleeting year!
What freezings have I felt, what dark days seen,
What old December's bareness everywhere!
And yet this time removed was summer's time,
The teeming autumn big with rich increase
Bearing the wanton burden of the prime,
Like widowed wombs after their lords' decease:
Yet this abundant issue seemed to me
But hope of orphans, and unfathered fruit;
For summer and his pleasures wait on thee,
And thou away, the very birds are mute;

Or if they sing, 'tis with so dull a cheer
That leaves look pale, dreading the winter's near.

From you have I been absent in the spring,
    When proud pied April, dressed in all his trim,
Hath put a spirit of youth in everything,
That heavy Saturn laughed, and leaped with him.
Yet nor the lays of birds, nor the sweet smell
Of different flowers in odour and in hue,
Could make me any summer's story tell,
Or from their proud lap pluck them where they grew;
Nor did I wonder at the lily's white,
Nor praise the deep vermilion in the rose;
They were but sweet, but figures of delight,
Drawn after you, you pattern of all those.
    Yet seemed it winter still, and, you away,
    As with your shadow I with these did play.

THE forward violet thus did I chide:
   'Sweet thief, whence didst thou steal thy sweet
      that smells,
If not from my love's breath? The purple pride
Which on thy soft cheek for complexion dwells
In my love's veins thou hast too grossly dyed.'
The lily I condemned for thy hand,
And buds of marjoram had stol'n thy hair;
The roses fearfully on thorns did stand,
One blushing shame, another white despair;
A third, nor red, nor white, had stol'n of both,
And to his robb'ry had annexed thy breath;
But for his theft, in pride of all his growth,
A vengeful canker ate him up to death.
  More flowers I noted, yet I none could see,
  But sweet, or colour, it had stol'n from thee.

WHERE art thou, Muse, that thou forget'st so long
　　To speak of that which gives thee all thy might?
Spend'st thou thy fury on some worthless song,
Dark'ning thy power to lend base subjects light?
Return, forgetful Muse, and straight redeem,
In gentle numbers, time so idly spent;
Sing to the ear that doth thy lays esteem,
And gives thy pen both skill and argument.
Rise, resty Muse: my love's sweet face survey,
If time have any wrinkle graven there;
If any, be a satire to decay,
And make time's spoils despised everywhere:
　　Give my love fame faster than time wastes life,
　　So thou prevent'st his scythe and crooked knife.

O TRUANT Muse, what shall be thy amends
   For thy neglect of truth in beauty dyed?
Both truth and beauty on my love depends;
So dost thou, too, and therein dignified:
Make answer, Muse, wilt thou not haply say,
'Truth needs no colour with his colour fixed,
Beauty no pencil, beauty's truth to lay,
But best is best if never intermixed'?
Because he needs no praise, wilt thou be dumb?
Excuse not silence so, for't lies in thee
To make him much outlive a gilded tomb,
And to be praised of ages yet to be.

   Then do thy office, Muse: I teach thee how
   To make him seem long hence as he shows now.

My love is strengthened, though more weak in
      seeming;
I love not less, though less the show appear.
That love is merchandised, whose rich esteeming
The owner's tongue doth publish everywhere.
Our love was new, and then but in the spring,
When I was wont to greet it with my lays,
As Philomel in summer's front doth sing,
And stops her pipe in growth of riper days.
Not that the summer is less pleasant now
Than when her mournful hymns did hush the night;
But that wild music burdens every bough,
And sweets grown common lose their dear delight:
   Therefore, like her, I sometime hold my tongue,
   Because I would not dull you with my song.

ALACK, what poverty my Muse brings forth,
That, having such a scope to show her pride,
The argument all bare is of more worth
Than when it hath my added praise beside.
O blame me not if I no more can write!
Look in your glass, and there appears a face
That overgoes my blunt invention quite,
Dulling my lines, and doing me disgrace.
Were it not sinful, then, striving to mend,
To mar the subject that before was well?
For to no other pass my verses tend
Than of your graces and your gifts to tell;
    And more, much more, than in my verse can sit
    Your own glass shows you, when you look in it.

To me, fair friend, you never can be old;
For as you were when first your eye I eyed,
Such seems your beauty still: three winters cold
Have from the forests shook three summers' pride;
Three beauteous springs to yellow autumn turned
In process of the seasons have I seen;
Three April perfumes in three hot Junes burned,
Since first I saw you fresh, which yet are green.
Ah, yet doth beauty, like a dial hand,
Steal from his figure, and no pace perceived;
So your sweet hue, which methinks still doth stand,
Hath motion, and mine eye may be deceived;
   For fear of which, hear this, thou age unbred,
   Ere you were born was beauty's summer dead.

Let not my love be called idolatry,
  Nor my beloved as an idol show,
Since all alike my songs and praises be,
To one, of one, still such, and ever so.
Kind is my love today, tomorrow kind,
Still constant in a wondrous excellence;
Therefore my verse, to constancy confined,
One thing expressing, leaves out difference.
Fair, kind and true is all my argument;
Fair, kind and true, varying to other words,
And in this change is my invention spent,
Three themes in one, which wondrous scope affords.
  Fair, kind and true have often lived alone,
  Which three, till now, never kept seat in one.

WHEN in the chronicle of wasted time
  I see descriptions of the fairest wights,
And beauty making beautiful old rhyme,
In praise of ladies dead, and lovely knights;
Then in the blazon of sweet beauties best,
Of hand, of foot, of lip, of eye, of brow,
I see their antique pen would have expressed
Even such a beauty as you master now:
So all their praises are but prophecies
Of this our time, all you prefiguring;
And for they looked but with divining eyes
They had not skill enough your worth to sing;
  For we which now behold these present days
  Have eyes to wonder, but lack tongues to praise.

Not mine own fears, nor the prophetic soul
Of the wide world, dreaming on things to come,
Can yet the lease of my true love control,
Supposed as forfeit to a confined doom.
The mortal moon hath her eclipse endured,
And the sad augurs mock their own presage;
Uncertainties now crown themselves assured,
And peace proclaims olives of endless age.
Now with the drops of this most balmy time
My love looks fresh, and death to me subscribes,
Since 'spite of him I'll live in this poor rhyme,
While he insults o'er dull and speechless tribes;

 And thou in this shalt find thy monument,
 When tyrants' crests and tombs of brass are spent.

WHAT'S in the brain that ink may character
    Which hath not figured to thee my true spirit?
What's new to speak, what new to register,
That may express my love, or thy dear merit?
Nothing, sweet boy; but yet, like prayers divine,
I must each day say o'er the very same,
Counting no old thing old; thou mine, I thine,
Even as when first I hallowed thy fair name:
So that eternal love, in love's fresh case,
Weighs not the dust and injury of age,
Nor gives to necessary wrinkles place
But makes antiquity for aye his page,
    Finding the first conceit of love there bred,
    Where time and outward form would show it dead.

O NEVER say that I was false of heart,
　　Though absence seemed my flame to qualify;
As easy might I from myself depart
As from my soul which in thy breast doth lie:
That is my home of love; if I have ranged,
Like him that travels I return again,
Just to the time, not with the time exchanged,
So that myself bring water for my stain;
Never believe, though in my nature reigned
All frailties that besiege all kinds of blood,
That it could so preposterously be stained,
To leave for nothing all thy sum of good:

　　For nothing this wide universe I call,
　　Save thou, my rose; in it thou art my all.

Alas, 'tis true, I have gone here and there,
    And made myself a motley to the view,
Gored mine own thoughts, sold cheap what is most
    dear,
Made old offences of affections new.
Most true it is that I have looked on truth
Askance and strangely; but by all above,
These blenches gave my heart another youth,
And worse essays proved thee my best of love.
Now all is done, save what shall have no end;
Mine appetite I never more will grind
On newer proof, to try an older friend,
A god in love, to whom I am confined:
    Then give me welcome, next my heaven the best,
    Even to thy pure and most most loving breast.

O FOR my sake do you with Fortune chide,
  The guilty goddess of my harmful deeds,
That did not better for my life provide
Than public means, which public manners breeds;
Thence comes it that my name receives a brand,
And almost thence my nature is subdued
To what it works in, like the dyer's hand;
Pity me, then, and wish I were renewed,
Whilst like a willing patient I will drink
Potions of eisell 'gainst my strong infection;
No bitterness that I will bitter think,
Nor double penance to correct correction.
  Pity me then, dear friend, and I assure ye,
  Even that your pity is enough to cure me.

❦ 112 ❧

Your love and pity doth th'impression fill
  Which vulgar scandal stamped upon my brow;
For what care I who calls me well or ill
So you o'er-green my bad, my good allow?
You are my all-the-world, and I must strive
To know my shames and praises from your tongue;
None else to me, nor I to none, alive,
That my steeled sense o'er-changes right or wrong.
In so profound abysm I throw all care
Of others' voices, that my adder's sense
To critic and to flatterer stopped are.
Mark how with my neglect I do dispense:
    You are so strongly in my purpose bred
    That all the world besides me thinks you're dead.

SINCE I left you, mine eye is in my mind,
    And that which governs me to go about
Doth part his function, and is partly blind;
Seems seeing, but effectually is out:
For it no form delivers to the heart
Of bird, of flower, or shape which it doth latch;
Of his quick objects hath the mind no part,
Nor his own vision holds what it doth catch:
For if it see the rud'st or gentlest sight,
The most sweet-favoured or deformed'st creature,
The mountain, or the sea, the day, or night,
The crow, or dove, it shapes them to your feature.
    Incapable of more, replete with you,
    My most true mind thus maketh mine untrue.

O R WHETHER doth my mind, being crowned
 with you,
Drink up the monarch's plague, this flattery?
Or whether shall I say mine eye saith true,
And that your love taught it this alchemy,
To make of monsters and things indigest
Such cherubins as your sweet self resemble,
Creating every bad a perfect best
As fast as objects to his beams assemble?
O, 'tis the first, 'tis flatt'ry in my seeing,
And my great mind most kingly drinks it up:
Mine eye well knows what with his gust is greeing,
And to his palate doth prepare the cup.

   If it be poisoned, 'tis the lesser sin,
   That mine eye loves it and doth first begin.

THOSE lines that I before have writ do lie,
  Even those that said I could not love you dearer;
Yet then my judgement knew no reason why
My most full flame should afterwards burn clearer.
But reckoning time, whose millioned accidents
Creep in 'twixt vows, and change decrees of kings,
Tan sacred beauty, blunt the sharp'st intents,
Divert strong minds to th' course of alt'ring things;
Alas, why, fearing of time's tyranny,
Might I not then say, 'Now I love you best',
When I was certain o'er uncertainty,
Crowning the present, doubting of the rest?
  Love is a babe; then might I not say so,
    To give full growth to that which still doth grow?

Let me not to the marriage of true minds
　　Admit impediments; love is not love
Which alters when it alteration finds,
Or bends with the remover to remove.
O no, it is an ever-fixed mark,
That looks on tempests and is never shaken;
It is the star to every wand'ring bark,
Whose worth's unknown, although his height be taken.
Love's not Time's fool, though rosy lips and cheeks
Within his bending sickle's compass come;
Love alters not with his brief hours and weeks,
But bears it out even to the edge of doom.
　　If this be error and upon me proved,
　　I never writ, nor no man ever loved.

Accuse me thus: that I have scanted all
  Wherein I should your great deserts repay,
Forgot upon your dearest love to call,
Whereto all bonds do tie me day by day;
That I have frequent been with unknown minds,
And given to time your own dear-purchased right;
That I have hoisted sail to all the winds
Which should transport me farthest from your sight.
Book both my wilfulness and errors down,
And on just proof surmise accumulate;
Bring me within the level of your frown,
But shoot not at me in your wakened hate:
    Since my appeal says I did strive to prove
    The constancy and virtue of your love.

Like as, to make our appetites more keen,
  With eager compounds we our palate urge;
As, to prevent our maladies unseen,
We sicken to shun sickness when we purge;
Even so, being full of your ne'er-cloying sweetness,
To bitter sauces did I frame my feeding,
And, sick of welfare, found a kind of meetness
To be diseased ere that there was true needing.
Thus policy in love, t'anticipate
The ills that were not, grew to faults assured,
And brought to medicine a healthful state
Which, rank of goodness, would by ill be cured;
  But thence I learn, and find the lesson true,
  Drugs poison him that so fell sick of you.

WHAT potions have I drunk of siren tears
    Distilled from limbecks foul as hell within,
Applying fears to hopes, and hopes to fears,
Still losing when I saw myself to win?
What wretched errors hath my heart committed,
Whilst it hath thought itself so blessed never?
How have mine eyes out of their spheres been fitted
In the distraction of this madding fever?
O benefit of ill: now I find true
That better is by evil still made better,
And ruined love when it is built anew
Grows fairer than at first, more strong, far greater:
    So I return rebuked to my content,
    And gain by ills thrice more than I have spent.

THAT you were once unkind befriends me now,
  And for that sorrow, which I then did feel,
Needs must I under my transgression bow,
Unless my nerves were brass or hammered steel:
For if you were by my unkindness shaken,
As I by yours, you've passed a hell of time,
And I, a tyrant, have no leisure taken
To weigh how once I suffered in your crime.
O that our night of woe might have remembered
My deepest sense how hard true sorrow hits,
And soon to you, as you to me then, tendered
The humble salve which wounded bosoms fits!
  But that your trespass now becomes a fee;
  Mine ransoms yours, and yours must ransom me.

❧ 121 ❧

'TIS better to be vile than vile esteemed,
    When not to be, receives reproach of being,
And the just pleasure lost, which is so deemed
Not by our feeling, but by others' seeing.
For why should others' false adulterate eyes
Give salutation to my sportive blood?
Or on my frailties why are frailer spies,
Which in their wills count bad what I think good?
No, I am that I am, and they that level
At my abuses, reckon up their own;
I may be straight, though they themselves be bevel.
By their rank thoughts my deeds must not be shown,
    Unless this general evil they maintain:
    All men are bad, and in their badness reign.

THY gift, thy tables, are within my brain
　　Full charactered with lasting memory,
Which shall above that idle rank remain
Beyond all date, even to eternity;
Or at the least, so long as brain and heart
Have faculty by nature to subsist;
Till each to razed oblivion yield his part
Of thee, thy record never can be missed.
That poor retention could not so much hold,
Nor need I tallies thy dear love to score;
Therefore to give them from me was I bold,
To trust those tables that receive thee more;
　　To keep an adjunct to remember thee
　　Were to import forgetfulness in me.

No! Time, thou shalt not boast that I do change;
　　Thy pyramids, built up with newer might,
To me are nothing novel, nothing strange;
They are but dressings of a former sight:
Our dates are brief, and therefore we admire
What thou dost foist upon us that is old,
And rather make them born to our desire
Than think that we before have heard them told:
Thy registers and thee I both defy,
Not wond'ring at the present, nor the past,
For thy records, and what we see doth lie,
Made more or less by thy continual haste:
　　This I do vow, and this shall ever be,
　　I will be true despite thy scythe and thee.

IF my dear love were but the child of state
    It might, for fortune's bastard, be unfathered,
As subject to time's love or to time's hate,
Weeds among weeds, or flowers with flowers gathered.
No, it was builded far from accident;
It suffers not in smiling pomp, nor falls
Under the blow of thralled discontent,
Whereto th'inviting time our fashion calls:
It fears not policy, that heretic,
Which works on leases of short-numbered hours,
But all alone stands hugely politic,
That it nor grows with heat, nor drowns with showers.
    To this I witness call the fools of time,
    Which die for goodness, who have lived for crime.

❧ 125 ❧

WERE'T ought to me I bore the canopy,
⠀⠀⠀With my extern the outward honouring,
Or laid great bases for eternity,
Which proves more short than waste or ruining?
Have I not seen dwellers on form and favour
Lose all, and more, by paying too much rent,
For compound sweet forgoing simple savour,
Pitiful thrivers, in their gazing spent?
No, let me be obsequious in thy heart,
And take thou my oblation, poor but free,
Which is not mixed with seconds, knows no art,
But mutual render, only me for thee.

⠀⠀*Hence, thou suborned informer, a true soul*
⠀⠀*When most impeached, stands least in thy control.*

O THOU my lovely Boy, who in thy power
   Dost hold time's fickle glass, his sickle hour,
Who hast by waning grown, and therein show'st
Thy lover's withering, as thy sweet self grow'st;
If nature, sovereign mistress over wrack,
As thou goest onwards still will pluck thee back,
She keeps thee to this purpose: that her skill
May time disgrace, and wretched minute kill.
Yet fear her, O thou minion of her pleasure:
She may detain, but not still keep, her treasure!
Her audit, though delayed, answered must be,
And her quietus is to render thee.

   (   )
   (   )

IN the old age black was not counted fair,
Or if it were, it bore not beauty's name;
But now is black beauty's successive heir,
And beauty slandered with a bastard shame:
For since each hand hath put on nature's power,
Fairing the foul with art's false borrowed face,
Sweet beauty hath no name, no holy bower,
But is profaned, if not lives in disgrace.
Therefore my mistress' eyes are raven black,
Her eyes so suited, and they mourners seem
At such who, not born fair, no beauty lack,
Sland'ring creation with a false esteem;
 Yet so they mourn, becoming of their woe,
 That every tongue says beauty should look so.

128

How oft when thou, my music, music play'st
Upon that blessed wood whose motion sounds
With thy sweet fingers, when thou gently sway'st
The wiry concord that mine ear confounds,
Do I envy those jacks that nimble leap,
To kiss the tender inward of thy hand,
Whilst my poor lips, which should that harvest reap,
At the wood's boldness by thee blushing stand?
To be so tickled they would change their state
And situation with those dancing chips,
O'er whom thy fingers walk with gentle gait,
Making dead wood more blessed than living lips.
  Since saucy jacks so happy are in this,
  Give them thy fingers, me thy lips to kiss.

TH'EXPENSE of spirit in a waste of shame
    Is lust in action; and till action, lust
Is perjured, murd'rous, bloody, full of blame,
Savage, extreme, rude, cruel, not to trust;
Enjoyed no sooner but despised straight;
Past reason hunted, and no sooner had,
Past reason hated as a swallowed bait,
On purpose laid to make the taker mad;
Mad in pursuit, and in possession so,
Had, having, and in quest to have, extreme;
A bliss in proof, and proved, a very woe;
Before, a joy proposed; behind, a dream.
    All this the world well knows, yet none knows well
    To shun the heaven that leads men to this hell.

My mistress' eyes are nothing like the sun;
Coral is far more red than her lips' red;
If snow be white, why then her breasts are dun;
If hairs be wires, black wires grow on her head;
I have seen roses damasked, red and white,
But no such roses see I in her cheeks;
And in some perfumes is there more delight
Than in the breath that from my mistress reeks.
I love to hear her speak, yet well I know
That music hath a far more pleasing sound;
I grant I never saw a goddess go;
My mistress when she walks treads on the ground.
   And yet, by heaven, I think my love as rare
   As any she belied with false compare.

❧ 131 ❧

T HOU art as tyrannous, so as thou art,
  As those whose beauties proudly make them cruel;
For well thou knowst, to my dear doting heart
Thou art the fairest and most precious jewel.
Yet in good faith some say, that thee behold,
Thy face hath not the power to make love groan;
To say they err, I dare not be so bold,
Although I swear it to myself alone;
And to be sure that is not false, I swear
A thousand groans but thinking on thy face;
One on another's neck do witness bear
Thy black is fairest in my judgement's place.
  In nothing art thou black save in thy deeds,
    And thence this slander, as I think, proceeds.

THINE eyes I love, and they, as pitying me,
   Knowing thy heart torment me with disdain,
Have put on black, and loving mourners be,
Looking with pretty ruth upon my pain;
And truly, not the morning sun of heaven
Better becomes the grey cheeks of the East,
Nor that full star that ushers in the even
Doth half that glory to the sober West
As those two mourning eyes become thy face:
O let it then as well beseem thy heart
To mourn for me, since mourning doth thee grace,
And suit thy pity like in every part:
   Then will I swear beauty herself is black,
   And all they foul that thy complexion lack.

❧ 133 ❧

Beshrew that heart that makes my heart to groan
For that deep wound it gives my friend and me;
Is't not enough to torture me alone,
But slave to slavery my sweet'st friend must be?
Me from myself thy cruel eye hath taken,
And my next self thou harder hast engrossed:
Of him, myself and thee I am forsaken,
A torment thrice threefold thus to be crossed.
Prison my heart in thy steel bosom's ward;
But then my friend's heart let my poor heart bail.
Whoe'er keeps me, let my heart be his guard;
Thou canst not then use rigour in my jail.
   And yet thou wilt, for I being pent in thee,
   Perforce am thine, and all that is in me.

So now I have confessed that he is thine,
    And I myself am mortgaged to thy will,
Myself I'll forfeit, so that other mine
Thou wilt restore to be my comfort still;
But thou wilt not, nor he will not be free,
For thou art covetous, and he is kind;
He learned but surety-like to write for me,
Under that bond that him as fast doth bind.
The statute of thy beauty thou wilt take,
Thou usurer, that put'st forth all to use,
And sue a friend, came debtor for my sake:
So him I lose through my unkind abuse.

   Him have I lost; thou hast both him and me;
   He pays the whole, and yet am I not free.

WHOEVER hath her wish, thou hast thy Will,
  And Will to boot, and Will in overplus;
More than enough am I, that vex thee still,
To thy sweet will making addition thus.
Wilt thou, whose will is large and spacious,
Not once vouchsafe to hide my will in thine?
Shall will in others seem right gracious,
And in my will no fair acceptance shine?
The sea, all water, yet receives rain still,
And in abundance addeth to his store;
So thou, being rich in Will, add to thy Will
One will of mine, to make thy large Will more:
  Let no unkind, no fair beseechers kill;
  Think all but one, and me in that one Will.

IF thy soul check thee that I come so near,
  Swear to thy blind soul that I was thy Will,
And will, thy soul knows, is admitted there;
Thus far for love my love-suit sweet fulfil.
Will will fulfil the treasure of thy love,
Ay, fill it full with wills, and my will one;
In things of great receipt with ease we prove
Among a number one is reckoned none.
Then in the number let me pass untold,
Though in thy store's account I one must be.
For nothing hold me, so it please thee hold
That nothing, me, a something sweet to thee.
  Make but my name thy love, and love that still;
  And then thou lov'st me, for my name is Will.

Thou blind fool love, what dost thou to mine eyes,
  That they behold, and see not what they see?
They know what beauty is, see where it lies,
Yet what the best is, take the worst to be.
If eyes, corrupt by over-partial looks,
Be anchored in the bay where all men ride,
Why of eyes' falsehood hast thou forged hooks,
Whereto the judgement of my heart is tied?
Why should my heart think that a several plot
Which my heart knows the wide world's common
        place?
Or mine eyes, seeing this, say this is not,
To put fair truth upon so foul a face?
  In things right true my heart and eyes have erred,
  And to this false plague are they now transferred.

WHEN my love swears that she is made of truth,
I do believe her, though I know she lies,
That she might think me some untutored youth
Unlearned in the world's false subtleties.
Thus vainly thinking that she thinks me young,
Although she knows my days are past the best,
Simply I credit her false-speaking tongue;
On both sides thus is simple truth suppressed.
But wherefore says she not she is unjust?
And wherefore say not I that I am old?
O love's best habit is in seeming trust,
And age in love loves not t' have years told:
    Therefore I lie with her, and she with me,
    And in our faults by lies we flattered be.

O CALL not me to justify the wrong
  That thy unkindness lays upon my heart;
Wound me not with thine eye, but with thy tongue;
Use power with power, and slay me not by art.
Tell me thou lov'st elsewhere; but in my sight,
Dear heart, forbear to glance thine eye aside.
What need'st thou wound with cunning, when thy
    might
Is more than my o'er‑pressed defence can bide?
Let me excuse thee: ah, my love well knows
Her pretty looks have been mine enemies,
And therefore from my face she turns my foes
That they elsewhere might dart their injuries.
  Yet do not so, but since I am near slain,
  Kill me outright with looks, and rid my pain.

❧ 140 ❧

Be wise as thou art cruel, do not press
My tongue-tied patience with too much disdain,
Lest sorrow lend me words, and words express
The manner of my pity-wanting pain.
If I might teach thee wit, better it were,
Though not to love, yet love to tell me so,
As testy sick men, when their deaths be near,
No news but health from their physicians know:
For if I should despair, I should grow mad,
And in my madness might speak ill of thee;
Now this ill-wresting world is grown so bad,
Mad slanderers by mad ears believed be.

    That I may not be so, nor thou belied,
    Bear thine eyes straight, though thy proud heart go wide.

In faith, I do not love thee with mine eyes,
　For they in thee a thousand errors note;
But 'tis my heart that loves what they despise,
Who in despite of view is pleased to dote.
Nor are mine ears with thy tongue's tune delighted,
Nor tender feeling to base touches prone,
Nor taste, nor smell, desire to be invited
To any sensual feast with thee alone:
But my five wits, nor my five senses, can
Dissuade one foolish heart from serving thee,
Who leaves unswayed the likeness of a man,
Thy proud heart's slave and vassal wretch to be:
　　Only my plague thus far I count my gain,
　　That she that makes me sin, awards me pain.

LOVE is my sin, and thy dear virtue hate,
 Hate of my sin, grounded on sinful loving;
O but with mine compare thou thine own state,
And thou shalt find it merits not reproving;
Or if it do, not from those lips of thine,
That have profaned their scarlet ornaments,
And sealed false bonds of love as oft as mine,
Robbed others' beds' revenues of their rents.
Be it lawful I love thee as thou lov'st those
Whom thine eyes woo, as mine importune thee,
Root pity in thy heart, that when it grows,
Thy pity may deserve to pitied be.
  If thou dost seek to have what thou dost hide,
  By self-example mayst thou be denied.

Lo, as a careful housewife runs to catch
　　One of her feathered creatures broke away,
Sets down her babe, and makes all swift dispatch
In pursuit of the thing she would have stay;
Whilst her neglected child holds her in chase,
Cries to catch her whose busy care is bent
To follow that which flies before her face,
Not prizing her poor infant's discontent:
So run'st thou after that which flies from thee,
Whilst I, thy babe, chase thee afar behind.
But if thou catch thy hope, turn back to me,
And play the mother's part, kiss me, be kind:
　　So will I pray that thou mayst have thy Will,
　　If thou turn back and my loud crying still.

Two loves I have, of comfort and despair,
    Which, like two spirits, do suggest me still:
The better angel is a man right fair,
The worser spirit a woman coloured ill.
To win me soon to hell my female evil
Tempteth my better angel from my side,
And would corrupt my saint to be a devil,
Wooing his purity with her foul pride;
And whether that my angel be turned fiend
Suspect I may, yet not directly tell;
But being both from me both to each friend,
I guess one angel in another's hell.

Yet this shall I ne'er know, but live in doubt,
Till my bad angel fire my good one out.

❦ 145 ❦

THOSE lips that love's own hand did make
 Breathed forth the sound that said 'I hate',
To me, that languished for her sake;
But when she saw my woeful state,
Straight in her heart did mercy come,
Chiding that tongue that, ever sweet,
Was used in giving gentle doom,
And taught it thus anew to greet:
'I hate' she altered with an end
That followed it as gentle day
Doth follow night, who like a fiend
From heaven to hell is flown away.
  'I hate' from 'hate' away she threw,
  And saved my life, saying 'not you'.

Poor soul, the centre of my sinful earth,
  Feeding these rebel powers that thee array,
Why dost thou pine within and suffer dearth,
Painting thy outward walls so costly gay?
Why so large cost, having so short a lease,
Dost thou upon thy fading mansion spend?
Shall worms, inheritors of this excess,
Eat up thy charge? Is this thy body's end?
Then soul, live thou upon thy servant's loss,
And let that pine to aggravate thy store;
Buy terms divine in selling hours of dross,
Within be fed, without be rich no more:

  So shalt thou feed on death, that feeds on men,
  And death once dead, there's no more dying then.

My love is as a fever, longing still
    For that which longer nurseth the disease,
Feeding on that which doth preserve the ill,
Th'uncertain sickly appetite to please:
My reason, the physician to my love,
Angry that his prescriptions are not kept,
Hath left me, and I, desperate, now approve
Desire is death, which physic did except.
Past cure I am, now reason is past care,
And frantic mad with ever more unrest;
My thoughts and my discourse as madmen's are,
At random from the truth vainly expressed:

For I have sworn thee fair, and thought thee bright,
Who art as black as hell, as dark as night.

O ME! What eyes hath love put in my head,
　　Which have no correspondence with true sight?
Or if they have, where is my judgement fled,
That censures falsely what they see aright?
If that be fair whereon my false eyes dote,
What means the world to say it is not so?
If it be not, then love doth well denote,
Love's eye is not so true as all men's: no,
How can it? O how can love's eye be true,
That is so vexed with watching and with tears?
No marvel then though I mistake my view:
The sun itself sees not, till heaven clears.
　　O cunning love, with tears thou keep'st me blind,
　　Lest eyes well seeing thy foul faults should find.

Canst thou, O cruel, say I love thee not,
  When I against myself with thee partake?
Do I not think on thee, when I forgot
Am of myself, all, tyrant, for thy sake?
Who hateth thee, that I do call my friend?
On whom frown'st thou, that I do fawn upon?
Nay, if thou lour'st on me, do I not spend
Revenge upon myself with present moan?
What merit do I in myself respect
That is so proud thy service to despise,
When all my best doth worship thy defect,
Commanded by the motion of thine eyes?
  But, love, hate on; for now I know thy mind:
  Those that can see thou lov'st, and I am blind.

O FROM what power hast thou this powerful might,
⠀⠀With insufficiency my heart to sway,
To make me give the lie to my true sight,
And swear that brightness doth not grace the day?
Whence hast thou this becoming of things ill,
That in the very refuse of thy deeds
There is such strength and warrantise of skill
That in my mind thy worst all best exceeds?
Who taught thee how to make me love thee more,
The more I hear and see just cause of hate?
O, though I love what others do abhor,
With others thou shouldst not abhor my state:
⠀⠀*If thy unworthiness raised love in me,*
⠀⠀*More worthy I to be beloved of thee.*

Love is too young to know what conscience is:
  Yet who knows not conscience is born of love?
Then, gentle cheater, urge not my amiss,
Lest guilty of my faults thy sweet self prove;
For, thou betraying me, I do betray
My nobler part to my gross body's treason;
My soul doth tell my body that he may
Triumph in love; flesh stays no further reason,
But rising at thy name doth point out thee
As his triumphant prize, proud of this pride:
He is contented thy poor drudge to be,
To stand in thy affairs, fall by thy side.
  No want of conscience hold it that I call
  Her 'love', for whose dear love I rise and fall.

❧ 152 ❧

I N loving thee thou knowst I am forsworn;
  But thou art twice forsworn to me love swearing,
In act thy bed‑vow broke and new faith torn,
In vowing new hate after new love bearing.
But why of two oaths' breach do I accuse thee,
When I break twenty? I am perjured most,
For all my vows are oaths but to misuse thee,
And all my honest faith in thee is lost:
For I have sworn deep oaths of thy deep kindness,
Oaths of thy love, thy truth, thy constancy,
And to enlighten thee gave eyes to blindness,
Or made them swear against the thing they see:

  For I have sworn thee fair: more perjured eye,
  To swear against the truth so foul a lie.

CUPID laid by his brand, and fell asleep;
A maid of Dian's this advantage found,
And his love-kindling fire did quickly steep
In a cold valley-fountain of that ground,
Which borrowed from this holy fire of love
A dateless lively heat still to endure,
And grew a seething bath, which yet men prove
Against strange maladies a sovereign cure:
But at my mistress' eye love's brand new fired,
The boy for trial needs would touch my breast;
I, sick withal, the help of bath desired,
And thither hied, a sad distempered guest,

But found no cure; the bath for my help lies
Where Cupid got new fire: my mistress' eye.

❧ 154 ❧

THE little love-god lying once asleep,
   Laid by his side his heart-inflaming brand,
Whilst many nymphs, that vowed chaste life to keep,
Came tripping by; but in her maiden hand
The fairest votary took up that fire
Which many legions of true hearts had warmed;
And so the general of hot desire
Was, sleeping, by a virgin hand disarmed.
This brand she quenched in a cool well by,
Which from love's fire took heat perpetual,
Growing a bath and healthful remedy
For men diseased; but I, my mistress' thrall,
   Came there for cure, and this by that I prove:
   Love's fire heats water, water cools not love.

FINIS

❧ A Lover's Complaint ❧

From off a hill whose concave womb reworded
A plaintful story from a sist'ring vale,
My spirits t'attend this double voice accorded,
And down I laid to list the sad-tuned tale;
Ere long espied a fickle maid full pale,
Tearing of papers, breaking rings a-twain,
Storming her world with sorrow's wind and rain.

※

Upon her head a plaited hive of straw,
Which fortified her visage from the sun,
Whereon the thought might think sometime it saw
The carcass of a beauty spent and done;
Time had not scythed all that youth begun,
Nor youth all quit, but spite of heaven's fell rage
Some beauty peeped through lattice of seared age.

※

Oft did she heave her napkin to her eyne,
Which on it had conceited characters,
Laund'ring the silken figures in the brine
That seasoned woe had pelleted in tears,
And often reading what contents it bears;
As often shrieking undistinguished woe,
In clamours of all size, both high and low.

❧

Sometimes her levelled eyes their carriage ride,
As they did batt'ry to the spheres intend;
Sometime, diverted, their poor balls are tied
To th'orbed earth; sometimes they do extend
Their view right on; anon their gazes lend
To every place at once, and nowhere fixed,
The mind and sight distractedly commixed.

❧

Her hair, nor loose, nor tied in formal plait,
Proclaimed in her a careless hand of pride;
For some untucked descended her sheaved hat,
Hanging her pale and pined cheek beside;
Some in her threaden fillet still did bide,
And, true to bondage, would not break from thence,
Though slackly braided in loose negligence.

❧

A thousand favours from a maund she drew,
Of amber, crystal and of beaded jet,
Which, one by one, she in a river threw,
Upon whose weeping margent she was set,
Like usury, applying wet to wet,
Or monarch's hands, that lets not bounty fall
Where want cries 'Some!', but where excess begs,
    'All!'

❧

Of folded schedules had she many a one,
Which she perused, sighed, tore and gave the flood;
Cracked many a ring of posied gold and bone,
Bidding them find their sepulchres in mud;
Found yet moe letters, sadly penned in blood,
With sleided silk, feat and affectedly
Enswathed and sealed to curious secrecy.

These often bathed she in her fluxive eyes,
And often kissed, and often gave to tear;
Cried, 'O false blood, thou register of lies,
What unapproved witness dost thou bear!
Ink would have seemed more black and damned
       here.'
This said, in top of rage the lines she rents,
Big discontent so breaking their contents.

A reverend man, that grazed his cattle nigh,
Sometime a blusterer, that the ruffle knew
Of court, of city, and had let go by
The swiftest hours observed as they flew,
Towards this afflicted fancy fastly drew,
And, privileged by age, desires to know
In brief the grounds and motives of her woe.

So slides he down upon his grained bat,
And comely distant sits he by her side,
When he again desires her, being sat,
Her grievance with his hearing to divide:
If that from him there may be aught applied
Which may her suffering ecstasy assuage,
'Tis promised in the charity of age.

'Father,' she says, 'though in me you behold
The injury of many a blasting hour,
Let it not tell your judgement I am old:
Not age, but sorrow, over me hath power.
I might as yet have been a spreading flower,
Fresh to myself, if I had self-applied
Love to myself, and to no love beside.

※

'But woe is me! Too early I attended
A youthful suit; it was to gain my grace;
O, one by nature's outwards so commended
That maidens' eyes stuck over all his face;
Love lacked a dwelling, and made him her place;
And when in his fair parts she did abide
She was new-lodged and newly deified.

※

'His browny locks did hang in crooked curls,
And every light occasion of the wind
Upon his lips their silken parcels hurls;
What's sweet to do, to do will aptly find;
Each eye that saw him did enchant the mind:
For on his visage was in little drawn
What largeness thinks in paradise was sawn.

❧

'Small show of man was yet upon his chin;
His phoenix down began but to appear,
Like unshorn velvet, on that termless skin,
Whose bare out-bragged the web it seemed to wear;
Yet showed his visage by that cost more dear,
And nice affections wavering stood in doubt
If best were as it was, or best without.

❧

'His qualities were beauteous as his form:
For maiden-tongued he was, and thereof free;
Yet if men moved him, was he such a storm
As oft 'twixt May and April is to see,
When winds breathe sweet, unruly though they be.
His rudeness so with his authorized youth
Did livery falseness in a pride of truth.

❧

'Well could he ride, and often men would say,
"That horse his mettle from his rider takes,
Proud of subjection, noble by the sway,
What rounds, what bounds, what course, what
    stop he makes!"
And controversy hence a question takes,
Whether the horse by him became his deed,
Or he his manage, by th' well-doing steed.

❧

'But quickly on this side the verdict went:
His real habitude gave life and grace
To appertainings and to ornament,
Accomplished in himself, not in his case;
All aids, themselves made fairer by their place,
Came for additions; yet their purposed trim
Pieced not his grace, but were all graced by him.

'So on the tip of his subduing tongue
All kind of arguments and question deep,
All replication prompt, and reason strong,
For his advantage still did wake and sleep,
To make the weeper laugh, the laugher weep:
He had the dialect and different skill,
Catching all passions in his craft of will.

'That he did in the general bosom reign
Of young, of old, and sexes both enchanted
To dwell with him in thoughts, or to remain
In personal duty, following where he haunted;
Consent's bewitched, ere he desire have granted,
And dialogued for him what he would say,
Asked their own wills, and made their wills obey.

'Many there were that did his picture get
To serve their eyes, and in it put their mind,
Like fools, that in th'imagination set
The goodly objects which abroad they find,
Of lands and mansions, theirs in thought assigned,
And labouring in moe pleasures to bestow them
Than the true gouty landlord which doth owe them.

'So many have, that never touched his hand,
Sweetly supposed them mistress of his heart:
My woeful self that did in freedom stand,
And was my own fee-simple, not in part,
What with his art in youth, and youth in art,
Threw my affections in his charmed power,
Reserved the stalk and gave him all my flower.

※

'Yet did I not, as some, my equals, did,
Demand of him; nor, being desired, yielded,
Finding myself in honour so forbid:
With safest distance I mine honour shielded.
Experience for me many bulwarks builded
Of proofs new-bleeding, which remained the foil
Of this false jewel and his amorous spoil.

※

'But ah! Who ever shunned by precedent
The destined ill she must herself assay,
Or forced examples 'gainst her own content,
To put the by-passed perils in her way?
Counsel may stop a while what will not stay:
For when we rage, advice is often seen
By blunting us to make our wits more keen.

'Nor gives it satisfaction to our blood
That we must curb it upon others' proof,
To be forebode the sweets that seems so good,
For fear of harms that preach in our behoof:
O appetite, from judgement stand aloof!
The one a palate hath that needs will taste,
Though reason weep and cry, "It is thy last!"

'For further, I could say, "This man's untrue",
And knew the patterns of his foul beguiling;
Heard where his plants in others' orchards grew;
Saw how deceits were gilded in his smiling;
Knew vows were ever brokers to defiling;
Thought characters and words merely but art,
And bastards of his foul adulterate heart.

'And long upon these terms I held my city,
Till thus he 'gan besiege me: "Gentle maid,
Have of my suffering youth some feeling pity
And be not of my holy vows afraid:
That's to ye sworn to none was ever said,
For feasts of love I have been called unto,
Till now, did ne'er invite, nor never woo.

' "All my offences that abroad you see
Are errors of the blood, none of the mind:
Love made them not; with acture they may be
Where neither party is nor true nor kind;
They sought their shame that so their shame did find,
And so much less of shame in me remains,
By how much of me their reproach contains.

❧

' "Among the many that mine eyes have seen,
Not one whose flame my heart so much as warmed,
Or my affection put to th' smallest teen,
Or any of my leisures ever charmed:
Harm have I done to them, but ne'er was harmed;
Kept hearts in liveries, but my own was free,
And reigned commanding in his monarchy.

❧

' "Look here what tributes wounded fancies
    sent me,
Of pallid pearls and rubies red as blood,
Figuring that they their passions likewise lent me
Of grief and blushes, aptly understood,
In bloodless white and the encrimsoned mood,
Effects of terror and dear modesty,
Encamped in hearts, but fighting outwardly.

' "And lo! Behold these talons of their hair,
With twisted metal amorously empleached,
I have received from many a several fair,
Their kind acceptance weepingly beseeched,
With th'annexions of fair gems enriched,
And deep-brained sonnets, that did amplify
Each stone's dear nature, worth and quality.

' "The diamond? Why, 'twas beautiful and hard,
Whereto his invised properties did tend:
The deep green emerald, in whose fresh regard
Weak sights their sickly radiance do amend;
The heaven-hued sapphire and the opal blend
With objects manifold; each several stone
With wit well-blazoned smiled, or made some moan.

※

' "Lo, all these trophies of affections hot,
Of pensived and subdued desires the tender,
Nature hath charged me that I hoard them not,
But yield them up where I myself must render,
That is, to you, my origin and ender:
For these of force must your oblations be;
Since I their altar, you empatron me.

※

' "O then advance of yours that phraseless hand,
Whose white weighs down the airy scale of praise;
Take all these similes to your own command,
Hallowed with sighs that burning lungs did raise:
What me, your minister for you, obeys,
Works under you; and to your audit comes
Their distract parcels in combined sums.

※

' "Lo, this device was sent me from a nun,
Or sister sanctified, of holiest note,
Which late her noble suit in court did shun,
Whose rarest havings made the blossoms dote;
For she was sought by spirits of richest coat,
But kept cold distance, and did thence remove
To spend her living in eternal love.

※

' "But O, my sweet, what labour is't to leave
The thing we have not, mast'ring what not strives,
Planing the place which did no form receive,
Playing patient sports in unconstrained gyves;
She that her fame so to herself contrives
The scars of battle 'scapeth by the flight,
And makes her absence valiant, not her might.

❧

' "O pardon me, in that my boast is true;
The accident which brought me to her eye
Upon the moment did her force subdue,
And now she would the caged cloister fly,
Religious love put out religion's eye;
Not to be tempted would she be immured,
And now to tempt all liberty procured.

❧

' "How mighty then you are, O hear me tell!
The broken bosoms that to me belong
Have emptied all their fountains in my well,
And mine I pour your ocean all among:
I strong o'er them, and you o'er me being strong,
Must for your victory us all congest,
As compound love, to physic your cold breast.

※

' "My parts had power to charm a sacred nun,
Who, disciplined, I dieted in grace,
Believed her eyes, when they t'assail begun,
All vows and consecrations giving place.
O most potential love! Vow, bond, nor space,
In thee hath neither sting, knot, nor confine,
For thou art all and all things else are thine.

※

' "When thou impressest, what are precepts worth
Of stale example? When thou wilt inflame,
How coldly those impediments stand forth,
Of wealth, of filial fear, law, kindred, fame?
Love's arms are peace, 'gainst rule, 'gainst sense,
     'gainst shame,
And sweetens in the suff'ring pangs it bears
The aloes of all forces, shocks and fears.

※

' "Now all these hearts that do on mine depend,
Feeling it break, with bleeding groans they pine,
And supplicant their sighs to you extend,
To leave the batt'ry that you make 'gainst mine,
Lending soft audience to my sweet design
And credent soul to that strong-bonded oath
That shall prefer and undertake my troth."

※

'This said, his wat'ry eyes he did dismount,
Whose sights till then were levelled on my face;
Each cheek a river running from a fount
With brinish current downward flowed apace.
O how the channel to the stream gave grace,
Who glazed with crystal gate the glowing roses
That flame through water which their hue encloses!

❧

'O father, what a hell of witchcraft lies
In the small orb of one particular tear!
But with the inundation of the eyes
What rocky heart to water will not wear?
What breast so cold that is not warmed here?
O cleft effect! Cold modesty, hot wrath,
Both fire from hence and chill extincture hath.

❧

'For lo, his passion, but an art of craft,
Even there resolved my reason into tears;
There my white stole of chastity I daffed,
Shook off my sober guards and civil fears,
Appeared to him as he to me appears,
All melting, though our drops this diff'rence bore:
His poisoned me, and mine did him restore.

🙚

'In him a plenitude of subtle matter,
Applied to cautels, all strange forms receives,
Of burning blushes, or of weeping water,
Or swooning paleness; and he takes and leaves
In either's, aptness, as it best deceives,
To blush at speeches rank, to weep at woes,
Or to turn white and swoon at tragic shows.

🙚

'That not a heart which in his level came
Could 'scape the hail of his all-hurting aim,
Showing fair nature is both kind and tame;
And veiled in them, did win whom he would maim.
Against the thing he sought he would exclaim;
When he most burned in heart-wished luxury
He preached pure maid, and praised cold chastity.

※

'Thus, merely with the garment of a grace,
The naked and concealed fiend he covered,
That th'unexperient gave the tempter place
Which, like a cherubin, above them hovered.
Who, young and simple, would not be so lovered?
Ay me, I fell, and yet do question make
What I should do again for such a sake.

※

'O, that infected moisture of his eye!
O, that false fire which in his cheek so glowed!
O, that forced thunder from his heart did fly!
O, that sad breath his spongy lungs bestowed!
O, all that borrowed motion, seeming owed,
Would yet again betray the fore-betrayed,
And new pervert a reconciled maid.'

❧ Index of First Lines ❧